Jam, Jelly & Jam Making Business Startup

HOW TO GROW A MILLION DOLLAR SUCCESS FROM HOME!

By

Samantha Parker

Copyrighted Material

Copyright © 2017 – **Valencia Publishing House**

All Rights Reserved.

No part of this publication may be reproduced, stored in a retrieval system or transmitted in any form or by any means, electronic, mechanical, photocopying, recording or otherwise without the proper written consent of the copyright holder, except brief quotations used in a review.

Published by:

www.Valenciapub.com

Valencia Publishing House
P.O. Box 548
Wilmer, Alabama 36587

Cover & Interior designed

By

Alex Lockridge

First Edition

TABLE OF CONTENTS

Part-1 9

How to Make Jam, Jelly & Pickles 9

Introduction 10

Steps You Need to Take to Get Started 14

Necessary Canning Supplies 19

    Water Bath Canner 19

    Pressure Canner/Cooker 20

    Canning Rack 21

    Jars 22

    Jar Lifter 22

    Magnetic Lid Lifter 23

    Wide Mouthed Canning Funnel 24

    Pectin 25

    Jelly Strainer 26

    Food Mill 27

Types of Canners 29

    Boiling Water Canners 30

    10 Steps to Using Boiling Water Canners 31

    Pressure Canners 33

    8 Steps to Using Pressure Canners 37

Sterilizing Jars 40

Checking Seals and Dealing with Issues 42

    Reprocessing 43

    Storing Canned Goods 44

    What to Do with Spoiled Food 45

- 8 Unsafe Canning Methods 48
  - Open Kettle Canning 48
  - Steam Canning 49
  - Micro-Dome Food Preserver 49
  - Solar Canning 49
  - Oven Canning 49
  - Microwave Processing 50
  - Dishwasher Processing 50
  - Aspirin/Salicylic Acid 51
- Canning Tips 52
- The Actual Jelly/Jam/Syrup Making Process 55
  - Four Essential Ingredients for Jams, Jellies & Syrup Making 55
  - Making Jellies, Syrups, and Jams 58
  - Difference between Jam & Jelly 60
- Pectin 62
  - Pectin Concentrations in Fruit 63
  - Testing for Pectin 65
  - How Much Pectin to Use 65
  - Converting from Liquid to Dry Pectin 65
  - Types of Pectin 66
  - Gelling Problems 68
    - Jam Too Stiff or Lumpy 68
    - Runny Jam 68
  - Fixing Jam/Jelly Batches 69
- Fruit Picking Tip Chart 72
- Fruit Storage Tip Chart 78
- Common Fruit pH Number Chart 81
- Fruit Yield Chart 85

Pickling 87

    Selecting Ingredients 88

    Reduced Salt Content Pickles 89

    Firming Agents 90

    Preventing Spoilage 91

    Choosing Cucumbers 91

    Low-Temperature Pasteurization Treatment 91

Part- 2 93

The Business 93

9 Steps to taking your Homemade Food Business to the Next Level ...94

    Business Structure 95

    Sole Proprietor 95

    Partnership 96

    Corporation (Inc. or Ltd.) 96

        S Corporation 97

        Limited Liability Company (LLC) 97

How and Where to Sell your Products 98

    Online 99

    Offline 102

    Selling Products to Gift Shops 104

        Research Potential Stores 105

        Choosing Consignment or Wholesale 105

        Have a Proposal 106

        Pitch Your Proposal 107

        Go To Trade Shows 107

    Selling Wholesale 108

Pricing Your Products 110

Marketing & Promoting your New Business 114
   Marketing Tips for Retail Stores 114
      Packaging 114
      Shelf Life 115
      Wholesale Marketing 115
      Retail Marketing 116
   Marketing Tips for Local Markets 116
      Flavors 116
      Stay Small 117

Part – 3 119
Legal & Safety Requirements 119

Legal Requirements 120
   Federal Food and Drug Administration (FDA) Regulations 120
   State and Local Laws 120
   Business Licensing 121
   Business Insurance 121
   Legal Advice 122
Meeting the Legal Requirements 123
   Local Health Department Issues 123
   Use a Commercial Kitchen for Food Preparation 124
   Food Safety Training 125
   Approved Recipes and Procedures 125
   Food Safety Procedures Plan, Critical Control Points, and Standard Operating Procedures 126
   Register with the State Health Authority 128
   Federal Approvals 128
Cottage Food Laws 130
   What Is the Cottage Food Law 130

    Why the Laws Exist 131

    What and Where You Can Sell 132

Labeling Requirements 135

    What to Include 135

    Special Labeling Requirements 136

Food and Workplace Safety 140

    Basic Sanitation and Safety 140

    Where to Get Food 142

    Selection, Storage, and Preparation of Ingredients 144

    Shelf Life of Ingredients 145

    Use of Frozen Foods 147

    Workplace Preparation 147

    Product Tracking 149

    Hand Washing 150

Last Words 153

Glossary 155

Recipes 163

    Pectin Recipe 163

    Apple Jelly Recipe 164

    Cherry Jam Recipe 168

    Cherry Jelly Recipe 171

    Fig Jelly Recipe 174

    Peach and Nectarine Recipe 177

    Pear Recipe 181

    Bread and Butter Pickle Recipe 185

    Fresh Pack Dill Pickles Recipe 187

    Sweet Gherkin Pickles Recipe 189

Quick Sweet Pickles Recipe 191

Reduced Sodium Sliced Sweet Pickles Recipe 193

Pickled Bread and Butter Zucchini Recipe 195

Pickled Asparagus Recipe 197

Pickled Carrots Recipe 198

Pickled Figs Recipe 200

PART-1

HOW TO MAKE JAM, JELLY & PICKLES

INTRODUCTION

I ALWAYS had a mini side hustle selling cookies, birthday cakes, homemade jams, and pickles that I made at home. But it was more of a hobby than anything. There were months when I made $400 and then there were months when I made as low as $70. But I didn't care; I enjoyed it. Then in 2008, my husband got laid off from the Ford plant. It was like the whole world just collapsed all around us, to make things even worse, we were in the middle of planning our youngest daughter's wedding.

We both knew at the age of 57 Bill will not have much luck finding a decent paying job in Detroit. It took us a good month to actually absorb the shock and for the reality to sink in. Then I decided I needed to step up and for the first time try to be the bread winner by selling the cookies, cakes, jams and pickers.

I knew a lady from our church who sold homemade brownies, but her's was an actual business unlike mine, I asked her for help and told her about our situation. She was an angle, she guided me through every step of the way, and in 3 months I started making enough income to support our family.

She taught me the followings:

Focus on only one type of product, not many (I was doing cookies, cakes, jams, pickles)

- Start from home
- Create a brand around your product
- Have a niche that makes you stand out from rest of the crowd
- Find out what flavors sell the most
- Create a line with no more than 5-7 SKU
- Market the product by taste test in local shops and markets

Well it sounds simple enough I am sure especially as I write this, but for me, the learning curve was a very steep one at first.

The angel lady's name is Betty, and she became my business partner after just a month and then came two other good news, Bill was called and hired back at the Ford plan again and our daughter's wedding went just as we expected maybe a little better than what we originally planned, thanks to my extra income.

In last seven years, we grew our business from 0 to $1.45 million dollars. We now have distribution throughout the country(mostly in various health food stores, Trader Joe's and Fresh Market stores nationwide). We recently received a decent purchase offer from a big brand food company and signed a contract to sell once their due diligence is complete. This is the very reason I am unable to mention our brand's name or any other details as that is part of the agreement we signed.

Okay, I am sure you didn't buy the book to hear my life story, it should all about you and your success. By the way, the very first thing she had me decide was if I was going to bake cakes or make Jams and Jellies, it was a tough call, but I picked Jams and jellies because of their shelf life and for the fact that it is much easier to package and display.

In this book I shared a lot of images, so you get a visual idea, I also shared a few YouTube videos of various processes, so it is easier for you to understand the individual process.

Okay, let's get started, Enjoy!

STEPS YOU NEED TO TAKE TO GET STARTED

IF YOU recall the five points I mentioned in the intro, that is where you need to get started.

My suggestion is to start small, start for under $500, so you can see how it does before you go spend a lot of money.

Let's go through the steps to see how ready you are.

Once you decided to get into this business, the first step is to create a brand for your products, a name that people can recognize you and your products with. Gather a few friends, brainstorm a few ideas and see which ideas stick and sound appealing. Once you decide on a brand, try to buy the domain name for that brand, just in case if your brand ever grows big you can take it national.

Once you decide on the name, you then would have to get a designer to design your logo and labels. This is an easy step, if you are on a tight budget, go to Fiverr.com and hire a logo and product label designer for $5 (make sure to hire someone with high positive ratings) and let hand this task. Now if you have around $150-$300 to spend, my suggestion is to go to www.99designs.com and post your job. Let many designers put in bids with a mock design. You pick the designer you like the best and let them do the work. This way you get a professionally done logo along with your labels that you will use on each jar

Next step is little more involved, in this step, you will need to do some market research. You need to find out a few things.

- A. How many other competitors will you be competing with locally
- B. How are their brand and packaging
- C. What is their pricing
- D. Where do they sell their products
- E. Is there any uniqueness about their product

Once you find these answers, then come up with a plan that would make you stand out from your competitors. Remember you have to have at least

USP (Unique selling proposition) about your products that will make you stand high above everyone else.

Otherwise, let's say there are three other sellers selling homemade jam and jellies in local farmer's markets, flea market and fruit stands, then you enter the same market, same stores with similar looking mason jars filled with strawberry, pear and apple jellies, just like the other competitors. Give me one reason why customers should pick your jam/jelly over the others, if you say it is because yours is cheaper, you are wrong! NEVER try to compete on the basis of price, it is a slippery slope, once you lower your price, your competitors will do the same, and before you know it, you will be losing money every time you sell a jar.

I can't tell you what your uniqueness should be, but I will tell you how we stood out from the rest. We stood out by making our whole line "Organic and Natural." Yes, we did paid little higher price to buy USDA certified organic fruits, but we did price our products higher too.

Here are few buzz words that can be your uniqueness but please make sure you follow what you put on your label.

- Non GMO (Meaning you used all non-GMO ingredients)
- All Natural
- Home Made
- Made from locally grown Fruits(Instead of using the work "locally" you can use your own city or state's name if appropriate)
- 100% Organic
- No Sugar Added
- Made With Pure Cane Syrup

Once you pass this hurdles, let's now figure out a line of products you need to have. Once again you need to come up with 5-7 SKU at the most. Your market research will tell you what flavors and items sell the most in your area. In our case, we started off with Apple, Strawberry, Pear and Apricot Jelly along with sweet and dill pickles.

Okay, as you can see you are almost to the finish line, all you have left to do is, make the actual products, label them, and present them to the local shops.

Remember just because you made some Organic jams and put them in 7 stores around town they will just fly off the shelves, unless you put some wings on each jar, they will not take off by themselves, this is when the hardest and longest process starts, Yes, I am talking about marketing.

I will touch on marketing in a separate chapter but remember an innovative marketing strategy can actually put wings on your jars, and they may just fly out of shelves, but a bad marketing campaign may just do the reverse.

NECESSARY CANNING SUPPLIES

THERE aren't that many supplies needed to get started with making homemade jams, jellies, and pickles. In fact, if you already preserve your food at home you probably already have the majority of these supplies. Here are the basics you need to can homemade food. But I will assume you never have, let me cover from A to Z this way everybody knows what we will need to get started.

WATER BATH CANNER

The water bath canner is essential for those who are going to be canning fruits, tomatoes, and any high-acid foods. The most common size is the 21 quart, but you can easily find larger versions if your business grows and you need to produce larger batches. If you are going to buy a used one make sure it has a lid and rack. Purchasing replacement racks for a water bath canner can often be the same price as a brand new canner.

PRESSURE CANNER/COOKER

(canningsupply.com)

A pressure canner is necessary if you are going to can vegetables, meats, seafood and other low-acid foods. These canners can reach 240 degrees Fahrenheit, the temperature needed to kill bacteria. Cost around $70.

CANNING RACK

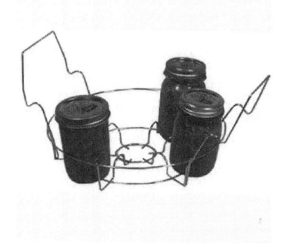

(Canningsupply.com)

Most canners come with a rack for the jars, but if yours didn't come with one, then you should purchase one separately. It is best to stick with a wire rack since plastic racks aren't as sturdy and won't hold as many jars.

JARS

If you are going to store food at room temperature, then you need to can them, and an essential supply for this is glass jars with lids and rings. Foods that will be stored in the refrigerator or freezer can be stored in glass or plastic freezer jars.

JAR LIFTER

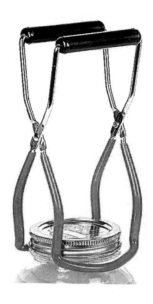

These are useful for safely lifting hot jars out of your canner after they've been processed. A necessary supply before you start canning.

MAGNETIC LID LIFTER

These help you to safely lift canning jar lids out of the boiling water after sterilizing. You can use a long-handled tong, but these magnetic ones are safer and will work much better, and they don't cost that much.

WIDE MOUTHED CANNING FUNNEL

These are a must since they will make it easier and faster to fill jars without all the mess. Simply place is on top of the jar and pour your ingredients. You can find them in both the stainless steel and plastic varieties. It is best to get the stainless steel option, they may cost a little more upfront, but you won't be replacing them as often.

PECTIN

Pectin is the necessary additive for jams and jellies to make them gel. It is naturally produced from citrus peels or apples. If you are going to be selling your homemade products, it is best to buy this in larger, multi-use containers. See the section on pectin to help you understand the difference between types of pectin and determine which one you want to use for your jam/jelly making.

JELLY STRAINER

This is a helpful tool to have if you're going to be producing a lot of jams/jellies. It makes it easier and cheaper to remove seeds and fruit pieces for a smoother finished jelly.

FOOD MILL

This isn't a necessary item for canning, but it can be a good investment. If you are going to make your own jams/jellies, then this will easily help you separate seeds and skins. It can also be used to strain jellies if needed.

Remember, when you are starting out from home on a budget, all the above items will not cost you more than $300, but when you start to grow big, you may want to start investing in more commercial grade equipment. I will touch more on that later.

TYPES OF CANNERS

WHEN it comes to heat processing home canned food, there are two types of canners to choose from. But if you are looking to start a business, you will have to use both forms of canning.

- **Boiling water canners**
- **Pressure canners**

Most canners are designed to hold seven-quart jars or eight to nine pints. There are some small pressure canners that hold only four-quart jars and some large pressure canners that can hold eighteen-pint jars in two layers or seven-quart size jars. My advice is to buy a larger size one.

A pressure canner is needed to process low-acid foods to get rid of botulism risks. While a pressure canner can also be used for acidic foods, boiling water canners are best for these foods because they are faster. A pressure canner will take 55 to 100 minutes to process a full load while processing acid foods in boiling water will vary from 25 to 60 minutes. This is because a boiling water canner needs about 20 to 30 minutes of heating to start boiling water.

On the other hand, a pressure canner needs 12 to 15 minutes of cooking before it vents, another 10 minutes to vent, another 5 minutes to pressurize the canner, another 8 to 10 minutes to process the food and lastly another 20 to 60 minutes to cool the canner before you can take out the jars.

Let's look at each type of canner and how to use them.

BOILING WATER CANNERS

Boiling water canners are either made of aluminum or porcelain-covered steel. They typically come with perforated, removable racks and a fitted lid. The canner needs to be deep enough for at least 1 inch of boiling water over the tops of the jars.

Some boiling water canners don't have a flat bottom, but this is necessary if you are going to be cooking on an electric stove. A flat or ridged bottom will work for a gas stove. For uniform cooking on an electric stove, you should choose a canner that is no more than 4 inches wider in diameter that the heating element.

Here is a YouTube Video on how Boiling Water Canner works

https://www.youtube.com/watch?v=gk5Dl84ADcQ

10 STEPS TO USING BOILING WATER CANNERS

If you are going to use a boiling water canner you will need to follow the following steps:

1. Before you start preparing your food, fill halfway with clean water. This is good for a load of pint jars. For other sizes and numbers of jars, the amount of water needs to be adjusted, so it is one to two inches over the top of the filled jars.

2. Preheat the water to 140 degrees Fahrenheit for raw-packed foods and 180 degrees Fahrenheit for hot-packed foods. While the water is preheating, you can start preparing your food.

3. Load your filled jars with fitted lids into the canner rack and then use the handles to lower it into the water. If you don't have a rack, you can

load one jar at a time with a jar lifter. If you use a jar lifter, you want to grasp securely below the neck of the jar and keep the jar upright at all times. Tilting the jar could result in food spilling into the sealing area of the lid.

4. If needed, add more boiling water to make sure it is at least one inch above the top of the jars. If you are going to be processing the jars for over 30 minutes, then you should make sure the water level is two inches above the tops of the jars.

5. Turn the heat up to high, cover the canner with the fitted lid and heat until the water is boiling continuously.

6. Set a timer for the total time required for the food to be processed.

7. Throughout the scheduled process you should keep the canner covered and maintain a boil. You can lower the heat setting just a little as long as a full boil is maintained during the entire process. If the water stops boiling at any time during the process, then you need to bring the water back to a

vigorous boil and begin the timing process from the start.

8. If needed, during the process you can add more boiling water to keep it above the top of the jars.

9. Once the jars have boiled for the appropriate time, turn off the heat and remove the fitted lid. Wait at least five minutes before removing the jars.

10. Using a jar lifter, remove the jars and place on a towel. Leave at least one inch between the jars when cooling. The jars should stay undisturbed to cool at room temperature for 12 to 24 hours.

PRESSURE CANNERS

In recent years, pressure canners for use in the home have been extensively redesigned. Pressure canners before the 1970s were a heavy-walled kettle with a clamp or turn on the lid. They often had a dial gauge, a vent port, and a safety fuse. Today, pressure canners are lightweight and thin-walled with a turn-on lid. They come with a jar rack, gasket, dial or weighted gauge, an automatic vent/cover lock, a vent port with a counterweight or weighted gauge and a safety fuse.

The pressure doesn't destroy microorganisms, but the high temperature used for an adequate period of time will destroy microorganisms. The success is based on the temperature of pure steam, free of air, at sea level. At sea level, pressure canners operated at a pressure of 10.5 pounds will reach an internal temperature of 240 degrees Fahrenheit. There are two main reasons a pressure canner won't obtain proper temperature:

1. At higher altitudes, internal canner temperatures are lower. To correct this, you need to operate canners at increased pressure for their appropriate altitude ranges.

2. Air trapped within a pressure canner will lower the temperature at 5, 10 and 15 pounds of pressure; resulting in under processing. The most air that becomes trapped in a canner occurs when processing raw-packed foods in a dial-gauge canner because these canners don't vent air during the process. To be safe, you should vent all pressure canners for 10 minutes before pressurizing.

To vent a pressure canner, you need to leave the vent port uncovered on newer models and manually open on older models. Once you notice steam escaping, set a timer for ten minutes. After this ten minutes of venting, close the petcock or place the counterweight or weight gauge over the vent port to begin pressurizing the canner.

If you have a weight-gauge model, they will exhaust tiny amounts of air and steam whenever the gauge rocks or jiggles during processing. This allows for precise control of pressure and doesn't require watching during processing or checking. You will know the canner is working and maintaining pressure by the sound of the weight rocking. The disadvantage of these models is that they can't precisely correct for higher altitudes.

Before each use of your pressure canner, you want to check dial gauges for accuracy. If a gauge reads high, it will result in under-processed and unsafe food. Low readings will result in overprocessing. If a gauge reads up to two pounds higher or lower, then adjustments can be made. Gauges that differ more than two pounds should be replaced.

You should handle canner lid gaskets carefully and clean them based on the manufacturer's directions. Gaskets that are nicked or dry rotted can allow steam to leak during pressurization. Between uses, you want to make sure to keep the gaskets clean. Some older models require a light coat of vegetable oil on the gaskets once a year. Newer model canners have pre-lubricated gaskets that don't need oiling. If you aren't sure about your model, then check the instructions.

Lastly, lid safety fuses are a thin metal insert or rubber plug designed to relieve excessive pressure from the canner. When cleaning the lids don't pick or scratch at the fuses if the unit has Underwriter's Laboratory (UL) approval to ensure safety. You can often get replacement gauges or other parts from stores that carry canning equipment or directly from the manufacturer.

Here is a YouTube Video on how Pressure Canner works

https://www.youtube.com/watch?v=A-fFAlldDKM

8 STEPS TO USING PRESSURE CANNERS

If you are going to use a pressure canner you will need to follow the following eight steps:

1. Place two to three inches of hot water in the canner. However, check the specific guide for your machine as some will require more water to start. Place filled jars on the rack with a jar lifter. Be sure to grab below the neck of the jar and keep the jar upright. Any tilting of the jar could result in food getting into the sealing of the lid. Fasten the canner lid securely.

2. Leave the weight off the vent port or open the petcock. Heat at the highest setting until you see steam flowing freely from the port or petcock.

3. While still maintaining the high heat setting, allow steam to flow continuously for 10 minutes and then place the weight on the vent port or close the petcock. For the next three to five minutes, the canner will now pressurize.

4. Once the pressuring reading on the dial gauge indicates the recommended pressure is reached, you can start the timing process. For some models,

this will be when the weighted gauge starts to jiggle or rock.

5. Regulate the heat as needed to maintain a steady pressure at or slightly above the correct gauge pressure. A quick or large variation during the process can cause liquid losses from the jars. If the pressure drops below the recommended amount at any time, then bring the canner back up to proper pressure and start the timing process again from the beginning. This is important to have safely processed food.

6. Once the timed process is finished, turn off the heat, remove the canner if possible and allow the canner to depressurize. Never force-cool the canner. This can result in unsafe food or spoilage. Opening the vent port before the canner is entirely depressurized will cause liquid loss from jars and seal failure.

7. If you have an older model without a dial gauge, you will need to time the depressurization. A heavy-walled canner will need about 30 minutes when loaded with pints and 45 minutes when loaded with quarts. A newer thin-walled canner will cool faster

and is equipped with a vent lock. Once the vent lock piston drops to a normal position on these newer models, the canners are depressurized.

8. Once depressurization is complete, remove the weight from the vent port or open the petcock. Wait another ten minutes then unfasten the lid and remove it carefully. Always lift the lid away from you, so the steam doesn't burn your face.

9. Remove the jars with a jar lifter and place on a towel. Space the jars one inch apart during cooling. Allow the jars to sit undisturbed at room temperature for 12 to 24 hours.

Once the jars have cooled, it is important that you check the seal and know how to deal with problems that may come up with jars that don't seal properly.

Before using a pressure canner, you want to make sure you properly sterilize and prepare your canning jars. Let's look at how best to do this.

STERILIZING JARS

IF YOU are going to can jams, jellies, and pickles you need to make sure you have properly sanitized canning jars. Most homemade foods are canned in 8-ounce jars. This is good since it means you don't need industrial sized cookware and you can easily sterilize several jars in a deep stock pot.

The most important thing to do before sterilizing is to inspect your jars. Make sure you see no chips or cracks. If everything looks okay, then you can start the sterilization process by cleaning the jars with warm, soapy water.

Place a wire rack into your stock pot and then fill with hot water to a level that will submerge all the jars by at least one inch. Place as many jars as you can fit on the rack, without crowding or allowing them to touch one another. Now bring the water to a boil. After the water has boiled, reduce the heat to a rolling simmer.

Many feel lids shouldn't be sterilized in this process because of the rubber rim. However, since you are making jams, jellies and pickles for resale you want to make sure you follow current USDA Canning Guidelines and these require you to sterilize lids in the same way as the jars.

After everything has been sterilized, you can remove the jars with stainless steel tongs and the lids with a magnetic grabber. Place the on a stable surface covered with a kitchen towel. You are now ready to add your jam, jelly or pickle ingredients.

CHECKING SEALS AND DEALING WITH ISSUES

MOST two piece lids that are commonly used for canning seal with a "pop" sound while cooling. This is because the lid is getting sucked down as a result of the vacuum created by the cooling and contracting contents inside the jar. Once the jars have cooled for 12 to 24 hours you can remove the screw bands and test the seals with one of the following three options:

1. Use a finger or thumb to press down on the middle of the lid. If the lid springs up when you release then the lid is unsealed.

2. Tap the lid with the bottom of a teaspoon. A clear ringing sound indicates a good seal. A dull sound means the lid is not sealed. A dull sound can also mean the food is in contact with the underside of the lid, which is neither a sign of a problem or spoilage. If sealed correctly, the jar will make a high-pitched ringing sound.

3. Look across the lid while holding it at eye level. The lid should be curved down slightly in the center. A lid that is either flat or bulging indicates the jar isn't sealed.

If a jar isn't sealed properly, you can refrigerate it and use the food within two to three days. Otherwise, you can reprocess the food within 24 hours or freeze the food.

REPROCESSING

12 to 24 hours after canning a jar will reach room temperature, and you can determine if the seal has failed. If the seal has failed, then you should remove the lid and check the sealing surface for any small nicks. If needed, you can change the jar or add a new and properly fitting lid. The food can them be reprocessed within 24 hours using the same time to process as you did before.

You may also want to adjust the headspace in unsealed jars to 1 and 1/2 inches. You can also choose to freeze jars instead of reprocessing. Single unsealed jars can be stored in the refrigerator and eaten within several days.

STORING CANNED GOODS

If the cooled jars have a properly tight vacuum seal, then you can prepare them for storage. Remove the screw bands and wash the jar to remove any food residue. Rinse and dry the jars. Place a label and date on the jars. They are best to be stored in a clean, cool, dark and dry place. Ideally, they should be stored between 50 and 70 degrees Fahrenheit. If you aren't canning to sell then you should only can what you'll be able to eat within a year.

Never store canned jars above 95 degrees Fahrenheit or near hot objects such as pipes, ranges or furnaces. You should never leave then in an uninsulated attic or places with direct sunlight. Under these type of conditions, the food loses quality in just a few weeks to months and can easily spoil.

Storing in damp areas can cause the metal lids to corrode, seals to break or recontamination and spoilage. Accidental freezing in cold conditions won't cause spoilage unless a jar becomes unsealed and contaminated.

However, freezing and thawing of canned food can cause it to soften. If you are going to store canned food in a place where they can potentially freeze then wrap them in newspapers, place in a heavy carton and cover with newspapers or blankets.

WHAT TO DO WITH SPOILED FOOD

You should never eat food from a jar with an unsealed lid, or that shows signs of spoilage. Spoilage is easily detected in jars with rings removed. The growth of bacteria and yeast that causes spoilage produces gas. This gas pressurizes the food, swelling the lid and breaking the jar seal. Before using canned food, examine the lid for tightness and vacuum. Lids with a concave center mean they are still sealed appropriately.

Next, hold the jar at eye level and rotate the jar to examine the outside surface. If there are streaks of dried food at the top of the jar, then check the contents for rising air bubbles or unnatural color.

Upon opening the jar, smell for any strange odors. Look for spurting liquid or cotton-like mold growth. Mold can either be white, blue, black or green.

Low acid foods will exhibit different signs of spoilage or may not even show much evidence. If you suspect any spoilage of food you should assume the spores have produced botulinum toxin and handle the food carefully in one of two ways:

1. If the jars are still sealed, place in a heavy garbage bag. Close the bag and place in the regular trash or bury in a landfill.

2. If you suspect the containers are unsealed, open or leaking, then you need to detoxify them before disposal.

The detoxifications process recommended by the USDA is as follows:

1. Place the suspect containers and lids on their sides in an 8-quart volume or larger stock pot, pan or boiling water canner.

2. Wash your hands completely.

3. Carefully add water to the pot and completely cover the containers with at least one inch above the containers. Avoid any splashing of water.

4. Place a lid on the pot and boil the water.

5. Boil for 30 minutes to ensure detoxification of the food and all components.

6. Cool the containers and then discard the container, lid, and food in the trash or bury in the soil.

7. Completely scrub all counters, containers, and equipment such as can opener, clothing, and hands. Anything that may have come in contact with the food or containers needs to be cleaned.

8. If you used any sponges or wash clothes in cleaning you should dispose of them by placing them in a plastic bag and then discarding in the trash.

It is also important that you know the unsafe methods of canning and preserving food. A lot of older recipes may still falsely refer to methods that are no longer considered safe. Let's look at some unsafe canning methods you shouldn't use.

8 UNSAFE CANNING METHODS

PEOPLE have as many thoughts and views on canning as there are possible canning methods. Although when it comes to canning, there are only two safe methods, the rest are unsafe ways to preserve and make homemade foods. Let's look at what methods of canning are unsafe and should never be used.

OPEN KETTLE CANNING

This is a process that involves placing hot food in jars and sealing them with no additional heat treatment. The idea is that after sealing the jar you place it upside down and it will seal once it cools.

However, this method isn't sterile since the contents were exposed to the air before sealing; exposing it to airborne bacteria. The bacteria is not exposed to high enough heat for a long enough period of time to destroy them. This is not a recommended way to preserve food.

STEAM CANNING

Steam canners were designed to process foods without the assistance of pressure. Manufacturers of this method claim the process requires less water and saves you time and energy. However, studies have shown that steam canners have lower temperature compared to proper canning methods. This method of canning will simply increase your risk of food spoilage.

MICRO-DOME FOOD PRESERVER

This food preservation equipment was recalled in August of 1987.

SOLAR CANNING

Using heat generated from captured sunlight is an unreliable method of processing acidic foods and should never be used as a way to process canned foods.

OVEN CANNING

This is a very hazardous practice. It involves placing jars in an oven and heating them. This method never heats above boiling point, and you aren't sure of uniform heat penetration so it shouldn't be a safe method for home canning. This process fails to kill most bacteria and can also explode due to the extreme heat.

MICROWAVE PROCESSING

A microwave cannot be used for canning. Microwave foods can only reach a maximum temperature of 212 degrees Fahrenheit with no uniform heating. You also have the added danger of the jars exploding as with the oven canning method.

DISHWASHER PROCESSING

This is another dangerous practice that should be avoided. The temperature of the water during the rinsing and cleaning cycles is below the required temperature to kill microorganisms. This results in under processed food that is unsafe to eat. It is okay to use the dishwasher to sterilize empty jars, especially if you have a sanitize setting. But it should never be used to process foods.

ASPIRIN/SALICYLIC ACID

These and other canning powders don't work as preservatives and don't replace proper heat processing for canned foods. These won't sufficiently acidify low acid foods. Low acid foods should only be processed in a pressure canner.

CANNING TIPS

IF YOU are going to start canning homemade jams, jellies and pickles then you should use the following tips to help you learn what you should and shouldn't do.

Never use overripe fruit. Canning doesn't improve food quality so if you start with low quality food it will only get worse as you store it.

Never add more low-acid ingredients other than those specified in the recipe. This can lead to an unsafe canned product.

Never add more seasonings or spices. These items are often high in bacteria and can cause a canned item to be unsafe.

Never add butter or fat. Unless you are using a tested recipe that calls for these, you shouldn't use them. Butters and fats don't store well and can increase food spoilage. Added butter or fat can also slow heat transfer and lead to an unsafe canned product.

Never thicken your canned foods with starches, flour, rice, barley or pasta. This applies to both soups and sauces as well as pickled items. Other than thickeners such as "Clear-gel" which has been approved and tested by the USDA; thickening items will absorb liquid during processing and slow the heating process. This leads to under processed and unsafe canned foods.

Never use jars larger than those specified in the recipes since you can get an unsafe product. It is usually okay to go smaller. In general, when canning you should never use anything larger than a quart jar.

Always add an acid such as lemon juice, vinegar or citric acid to tomato products per the recipe instructions. Food scientists proved through research in 1994 that the risk of botulism poisoning is reduced when acid is added to canned tomatoes. If you don't prefer the tart taste of acids, you can balance them by adding sugar.

Always heat process your canned foods. You may find people advising otherwise or see different methods mentioned in recipes. However, as we stated earlier, you should only use one of the two approved canning methods to make your food safe.

Always increase you water bath processing times when you are at an altitude of 1,000 feet or more.

Always use standard canning jars in your process. Commercial foods jars that aren't heat tempered can easily break. Even with official canning jars, make sure you discard them if you notice any chips, cracks, dents or rust. Defects will prevent airtight seals can lead to unsafe food.

Always use flat lids only once. The screw bands and the jars can be reused as long as they are in good condition and properly sterilized.

Always check jars for sealing within 24 hours of canning. If a jar fails to seal properly, you should refrigerate it and use the food as soon as possible, treating it as fresh food.

If you have scale or hard water films on your jar, soak them for several hours in a solution of 1 cup vinegar per gallon of water.

THE ACTUAL JELLY/JAM/SYRUP MAKING PROCESS

FOUR ESSENTIAL INGREDIENTS FOR JAMS, JELLIES & SYRUP MAKING

1. Fruit

- Provides unique flavor and characteristic color as well as some pectin and acid.
- Overripe fruit should be used with caution in products without added pectin as they have less natural pectin.
- Use fruit free from spoilage and mold. Some irregularly shaped and imperfect fruit can be used. In addition, canned or frozen fruit can be used for making jelly.

2. Pectin

- Pectin is found naturally in fruits, and this is the ingredient, when combined with sugar or other

sweeteners (but NOT artificial sweeteners), that causes the fruit to gel.
- Pectin is concentrated in the skins and cores of fruits. This is why recipes often call for using skins and cores for juicing or pulping.
- Commercial pectin comes in liquid and powdered form but is not interchangeable in recipes. Be sure to follow the recipes and instructions accurately.
- Reduced-sugar jams and jellies along with no-added sugar jams and jellies use different commercial pectin. Follow directions carefully.

3. Acid

- Acid is necessary for gel formation and flavor.
- Fruits naturally contain acid, but the amount of acid varies with the fruit and degree of ripeness.
- It is important to follow recipe directions carefully to determine if additional acid is needed for the specific fruit being preserved.

4. Sweeteners

- Sugar is essential to help form the gel and contributes to flavor and taste. The type of

sugar used in recipes most often is granulated white sugar.
- Use the specific amount of sugar called for in the recipe. The amount of sugar must be in proper proportion with pectin and acid to make a good gel. Reducing the amount of sugar in the recipe contributes to poor gelling or the lack of gelling.
- Other types of sweeteners, such as honey or reduced-calorie sugars, can be used. It is important to use recipes that have been tested using these sweeteners. If you want to make jam or jelly with no added sugar, use a specially modified commercial pectin.
- Light corn syrup or light, mild honey can be used to replace the part, but not all, of the sugar. The flavor will be slightly different. However, it is best to use recipes calling for honey or corn syrup rather than substituting these sweeteners for sugar.
- Brown sugar, sorghum, and molasses are not recommended since their flavor overpowers the fruit flavor.

MAKING JELLIES, SYRUPS, AND JAMS

1. **Prepare the fruit**. Wash fruit and discard caps, stems and damaged portions, but do not remove the skin or cores, since natural pectin found in fruit is concentrated in these parts.

2. **Cook the Fruit.** Cook the fruit slowly with enough water to cover it. Fruit should never float in the pan. Simmer for at least 45 minutes, should be very soft. Extra water can be added, if necessary to prevent burning.

3. **Pulp vs. Juice.** Put the pulp into a jelly bag and strain the juices into a bowl.

4. **Add Pectin.** A rule of thumb is that One pound of fruit should yield at least one cup of broth/ juice, and for every 4 cups of juice you add around 3.5 cups of sugar, but again it will vary by what fruit you use and what is the pectin content of that fruit. So just follow the recipe

5. **Add Sugar.** Bring your juice to a boil, remove from heat then add sugar, stir until dissolved, boil again till the setting point is reached

6. **Clean the Top.** Skim Off any and all surface foam and scum with a slightly dampened paper towel.

7. **Pour into Jars.** Be careful when pouring so you can prevent bubbles from forming.

8. **Seal the top.** Seal the top, so it is airtight and ready for sale.

Fresh fruits and juices, as well as commercially canned or frozen fruit juice, can be used with commercially prepared powdered or liquid pectin. The order of combining ingredients depends on the type of pectin used.

Jelly, syrup or jam made with added pectin requires less cooking and generally gives a larger yield. In addition, using added pectin eliminates the need to test hot jellies and jams for proper gelling. Adding ¼ teaspoon of butter or margarine with the juice and pectin will reduce foaming.

Purchase fresh pectin each year; check the date on the box or bottle, as old pectin may result in poor gels. Follow all directions carefully.

Here is a YouTube video I found that shows how someone made apple jelly at home, take a look, it is really a rather simple process.

https://www.youtube.com/watch?v=ZI5LxrcVlKU

Here is another YouTube video showing how to make jelly from store bought juice, take a look

https://www.youtube.com/watch?v=BQ3GNBF3uH4

DIFFERENCE BETWEEN JAM & JELLY

All jams and jellies are made from fruit mixed with sugar, pectin, and acid, but the difference between them comes in the form that the fruit takes in the finished product.

In Jam, the fruit comes in the form of pulp or crushed, so they are naturally less stiff is easier to spread.

In Jelly, the fruit comes in the form of juice, so they are more transparent in color and stiffer than jams.

PECTIN

PECTIN is a substance that naturally occurs in berries, apples and other fruit. When this pectin is heated with sugar, it causes the thickening that is typically found in jams and jellies.

Before pectin, people used to cook the jam until all the vitamins were gone and the fruit was cooked down to a thicker consistency. At the end of this book, I added a recipe if you want to make your own pectin. However, using packaged pectin is safe and natural. Packaged pectin comes from apples with a little bit of citric acid and dextrose as binders; nothing that will change the flavor. The pectin simply helps thicken and allows you to use less sugar when cooking. For our business, we buy packaged apple based pectin and don't make our own.

The pectin you buy at the store is typically produced in Europe and imported into the US. It does have a limited shelf life so you shouldn't keep it beyond a year. After a year it will have a decreased ability to gel.

PECTIN CONCENTRATIONS IN FRUIT

Fruit can be found in three groups based on their pectin content. These groups are as follows:

Group 1 - If the fruit isn't overripe, then it typically has enough natural pectin and acid for gel formation with only sugar added.

Group 2 - These fruits are low in natural acid or pectin and often need either acid or pectin added.

Group 3 - These are fruits that always need acid, pectin or both added.

Fruits in the various groups include the following:

Group 1	Group 2	Group 3
Sour Apples	Ripe Apples	Apricots
Sour Blackberries	Ripe Blackberries	Blueberries
Crab Apples	Sour Cherries	Sweet Cherries
Cranberries	Chokecherries	Figs
Currants	Elderberries	Western Concord Grapes

Gooseberries	All but Concord Grapes	Bottle Grape Juice
Eastern Concord Grapes	Loquats	Grapefruit
Lemons		Guavas
Loganberries		Nectarines
Plums (not Italian)		Peaches
Quinces		Pears
Raspberries		Italian Plums
Citrus Skins		Oranges
		Pomegranates
		Strawberries

The pectin content in fruit is often higher when the fruit is barely ripe and diminishes once the fruit matures from fully ripe to overripe. The ripening process breaks down pectin, which causes the fruit to soften as it becomes ripe. Apples and Crab Apples, especially the unripe ones, are a good source of pectin which is why they are often used for making commercial pectin. A few commercial pectin are made from citrus peels.

TESTING FOR PECTIN

If you need there is a way to test for the amount of pectin in the fruit. Mix 1 teaspoon of the cooked, cooled and crushed fruit with 1 tablespoon of rubbing alcohol in a closed container. Shake gently. The juice that is high in pectin will form a solid gelatinous lump. The juice that is low in pectin will only form small rubbery particles. An average pectin content results in a few pieces of jelly-like substance. Obviously discard after testing and don't eat anything mixed with rubbing alcohol.

HOW MUCH PECTIN TO USE

In order to allow jams and jellies to set your pectin needs the appropriate acidity and sugar ratio. These proportions are going to vary based on the fruit you are using. This is why you want to carefully follow the recipe you are using.

CONVERTING FROM LIQUID TO DRY PECTIN

If a recipe calls for a pouch of liquid pectin, you can substitute for dry pectin. The average dry pectin comes in a box of 1.75 ounces per packet. This is the same amount as one pouch of liquid pectin. If you have bulk pectin, then one packet is slightly less than 1/2 cup by volume. So you can use a little less than 1/2 cup to equal a pouch of liquid pectin.

TYPES OF PECTIN

There are several types of pectin. Consider the following table to determine which type of pectin is best for you:

Type of Pectin	Pros	Cons
Liquid	Already Dissolved	Costs More Messier Doesn't Keep Once Opened
Regular Dry	None	Has A Lot of Added Sugar
Lower Sugar Dry	Uses 40% Less Sugar	None
No Sugar Dry	No Sugar Needed	If no sugar is used the jam

	You Can Add Stevia, Splenda or Fruit Juice	won't be as bright and will be runnier.
None	Cheaper	More Sugar Needed
		Longer Cook Time
		Lower Nutritional Value
Frozen Jam Pectin	No Cooking	Must Be Stored in the Freezer
		Doesn't Always Set Well
Low Methoxyl Pectin Sugar	No Sugar Required	Doesn't Have as Good Clarity
	Good for Pepper or Mint Jelly	Difficult to Find
	You Can Use Low or No Calorie Sweeteners	
	Cheaper	
Modified Citrus Pectin	Believed to Have Anti-Cancer Properties	Difficult to Find
	Reliable for	

| | Low and No Sugar Jams | |

GELLING PROBLEMS

JAM TOO STIFF OR LUMPY

If too much pectin is used, the gel formation will be too strong causing the jam to become stiff, lumpy or granular in texture.

Jam can be too stiff if it is cooked too long at a lower temperature since the water boils off and the pectin isn't broken down effectively.

Jam that is cooked too high for too long or not stirred frequently enough.

Using under-ripe fruit in the recipe, which has more pectin.

RUNNY JAM

Too little pectin or sugar can lead to a runny jam. Also if you undercook it.

Overheating or uneven heat distribution. Often happens when trying to make double batches.

FIXING JAM/JELLY BATCHES

If your jam/jelly comes out too runny or too thick, you can fix it without wasting your batch.

For thick jam/jelly, you simply need to heat one or two cups of fruit juice to boiling and then gradually pour into the jam/jelly until the desired consistency is reached. Then you simply go about the canning process.

If your jam/jelly is runny, then you will need to have a few more steps to fix the problem. Consider the instructions below for solving this issue.

Ingredients:

- Jam/jelly to be remade.
- No sugar needed pectin.
- Lemon juice.
- Sugar.

You are also going to need new lids for your jars. You can reuse the rings and wash out the jars.

Directions:

1. You need to determine how much jam/jelly you need to remake. Measure the amount to be recooked. It is best to only work with four to six cups at a time. Add up the volume of all jars to be reworked to determine the size of your batch in quarts. Once you know how much you can open all the jars and dump them into a large pot. You can place the emptied jars in the dishwasher, so they'll be ready to reuse later.

2. For each quart of jam/jelly, you need to fix you should mix 1/4 cup sugar, 1/4 cup water or white grape juice, 2 tablespoons lemon juice and 4 teaspoons powdered pectin in a large pot.

3. Mix the jam/jelly into the pectin mixture and bring to boil over high heat while stirring constantly. You should never make a batch of jam/jelly over six cups of crushed fresh or frozen fruit and never remake a batch over 2.5 quarts. This is because it can cause non-uniform heating resulting in some pectin getting over cooked and

others undercooked. This is the main reason why jam/jelly doesn't set. After the mix is boiling, cook for 1 minute.

4. To test for the thickness, you should leave a metal tablespoon in a glass of ice water Shake off the water and then scoop a half spoonful of the mix. Allow it to cool to room temperature in about a minute or so. If it thickens to a consistency you like, then the jam/jelly is ready. If not you may need to add more pectin and bring it to a boil for another minute.

5. Remove from the heat and quickly skim the foam off the top. Fill your sterile jars, leaving 1/4 inch of headspace. Adjust new lids and can according to instructions.

Before you go out and start canning food, take a look at the following tips to help you have a smooth and successful process.

FRUIT PICKING TIP CHART

Fruit	When to Pick
Apple	❖ Based upon condition and maturity. Early indication is when normal unblemished fruit starts to drop. Check to see if the flesh color at the bottom has turned from green to yellow-green. ❖ When all signs of maturity are present, an Apple will be easy to pick with the stem still attached to the fruit. ❖ Pick by rolling or twisting the apple away from the fruit spur.
Apricot	❖ Needs to be firm-ripe on the tree. ❖ Should be soft, golden yellow and easily separated from the stem.
Blackberry	❖ When it is soft and sweet, almost dropping off at the slightest touch.

	❖ Pick early in the day since these don't spoil as quickly.
Blueberry	❖ Pick when uniform in color and easily coming loose from the plant. ❖ A reddish ring around the indentation where the fruit attaches to the stem indicates it is not ripe. ❖ Pick by gently rolling each one from the cluster with the thumb into the palm of the hand.
Cherries	❖ Pick when at their maximum size and full-flavored. ❖ Become firm when ripe and will part easily from the stem. ❖ Pick when they have a shiny skin and fresh stem.
Currant	❖ Pick when firm, but not quite ripe. ❖ Twist the cluster from the branch first, then strip the berries from the cluster.

Elderberry	❖	Pick when half ripe.
	❖	Pick as clusters and not individual berries.
Figs	❖	In the US, they often peak from July to Frost in the South and August or later in the North.
Gooseberry	❖	Pick in the green or immature stage, but after they reach full size.
	❖	Pick when pinkish in color for a sweeter flavor.
	❖	Pick as individual berries or strip them off the stem later.
Grape	❖	Color and flavor indicate ripeness.
	❖	The natural bloom is noticeable at the fully-ripe stage, and the berries are slightly less firm.
	❖	Cut each cluster from the vine and handle as little as possible.
Nectarine	❖	A creamy-yellow background color

	indicates ripeness.
	❖ They will yield slightly to pressure, especially along the seam.
	❖ Pick with a slight twist to remove from the stem.
Peach	❖ Pick when the fruit easily separates from the twigs.
	❖ Pick when the ground color goes from green to yellow.
	❖ A yellow-flesh variety ripens to an orange color, and a white-flesh variety ripens to a greenish to yellow-white color.
Pear	❖ Pick early and allow to ripen indoors.
	❖ There will be a change in color from green to yellow, and the stem will separate easily from the branch.
	❖ To pick, grasp the pear firmly and twist or roll to make the stem separate from the tree.

Plum	❖ As a plum matures, the color changes noticeably. With blue or purple varieties, the color goes from green to greenish-blue or reddish-purple to a dark blue or purple. In other varieties, the color goes from a yellowish-green to a more definite yellow or straw yellow and then to a yellow or red. ❖ As color increases the flesh becomes soft at the tip end. ❖ Can be picked when slightly under-ripe for preserve.
Raspberry	❖ When ripe they will easily separate from the plant. ❖ Should be picked every two to three days. ❖ Use thumb, index and middle fingers to pick the berries.
Strawberry	❖ Pick with three-fourths red. ❖ Pick early in the morning and with

	the stem attached.
	❖ Grabbed the stem with the thumb and forefinger to pinch.

Once you pick the fruit, unless you are going to turn it into jam/jelly right away, you are going to need to make sure you store it properly. Consider the following table to see how to store the most common fruit used in making jam/jelly.

FRUIT STORAGE TIP CHART

Fruit	Storage Tips
Apple	✧ Keep cool at 33-35 degrees Fahrenheit in order to retain flavor and quality. ✧ At 40 degrees Fahrenheit, they ripen slowly. ✧ At 60 degrees Fahrenheit, they mature rapidly. ✧ Best to store in the refrigerator in perforated plastic bags.
Apricot	✧ Stored at 40 to 50 degrees Fahrenheit they will keep for three weeks.
Blackberry	✧ Stored in a cool place, they will keep for several days.
Blueberry	✧ Cool to 35 degrees Fahrenheit as soon as possible after picking and they'll be good for a week.

Cherries	✧	They will keep longer if the stems are attached.
	✧	Store in the refrigerator for two to three days.
Grapes	✧	Store in a cool, well-ventilated place and they will keep for several weeks.
	✧	Keep away from other produce since they absorb odors.
Nectarine	✧	At 30 degrees Fahrenheit and high humidity, they can be stored for three to four weeks.
Peach	✧	Store at 32 degrees Fahrenheit and high humidity.
Pear	✧	Should be ripened at 60 to 70 degrees Fahrenheit.
	✧	Freshly picked pears will stay longer in the refrigerator.
Plum	✧	At 30-32 degrees Fahrenheit, they can be stored for two to four

		weeks.
Raspberry	✧	Handle as little as possible and keep in the shade until you can place in cool storage.
	✧	Ideal conditions are 31-32 degrees Fahrenheit and 90-95% humidity. Under these conditions they will keep for a day or two.
Strawberry	✧	Should be processed soon after picking.
	✧	Kept below 40 degrees Fahrenheit and at an 85-90% humidity.

It is also important to understand the pH of your fruits as I've already talked about at the start of the canning process. Here are the most common.

COMMON FRUIT PH NUMBER CHART

Fruit	pH
Apple Juice	3.35-4.00
Apple Sauce	3.10-3.60
Apples Baked with Sugar	3.20-3.55
Apples	3.30-4.00
Red Delicious Apples	3.90
Golden Delicious Apples	3.60
Jonathan Apples	3.33
McIntosh Apples	3.34
Wine sap Apples	3.47
Fresh Apricots	3.30-4.80
Canned Apricots	3.40-3.78
Dried & Stewed Apricots	3.30-3.51
Apricot Nectar	3.78
Pureed Apricots	3.42-3.83
Washington Blackberries	3.85-4.50
Maine Blueberries	3.12-3.33
Frozen Blueberries	3.11-3.22

California Cherries	4.01-4.54
Frozen Cherries	3.32-3.37
Black Canned Cherries	3.82-3.93
Maraschino Cherries	3.47-3.52
Red Water Packed Cherries	3.25-3.82
Royal Ann Cherries	3.80-3.83
Calamyrna Figs	5.05-5.98
Canned Figs	4.92-5.00
Gooseberries	2.80-3.00
Canned Grapes	3.50-4.50
Concord Grapes	2.80-3.00
Lady Finger Grapes	3.51-3.58
Malaga Grapes	3.71-3.78
Niagara Grapes	2.80-3.27
Ribier Grapes	3.70-3.80
Seedless Grapes	2.90-3.82
Tokyo Grapes	3.50-3.84
Peaches	3.30-4.05
Canned Peaches	3.70-4.20
Peaches Cooked with Sugar	3.55-3.72

Frozen Peaches	3.28-3.35
Bartlett Pears	3.50-4.60
Canned Pears	4.00-4.07
Sickle Pears Cooked with Sugar	4.04-4.21
Pear Nectar	4.03
Fresh Pack Pickles	5.10-5.40
Plum Nectar	3.45
Blue Plums	2.80-3.40
Damson Plums	2.90-3.10
Frozen Plums	3.22-3.42
Green Gage Plums	3.60-4.30
Canned Green Gage Plums	3.22-3.32
Red Plums	3.60-4.30
Spiced Plums	3.64
Yellow Plums	3.90-4.45
Raspberries	3.22-3.95
Frozen Raspberries	3.18-3.26
New Jersey Raspberries	3.50-3.82
Strawberries	3.00-3.90
California Strawberries	3.32-3.50

| Frozen Strawberries | 3.21-3.32 |

Lastly, I want to provide you with some information on how much fruit you should pick so you can adequately fill your order needs without having too much fruit laying around going to waste.

FRUIT YIELD CHART

Fruit	Amount of Fresh Fruit	Common Products	Amount of Canned	Amount of Frozen
Apples	42-48 lbs.	Sauce or Juice	12-16 Quarts	28-36 pints
Apples	3 lbs.	Sauce	1 Quart	2 Pints
Apples	8 Medium Apples = 2.25 lbs.	Sauce or Pie	3 Cups	
Berries (except Strawberries)	24 Quart Crate	Jams, Jellies	12-18 Quarts	32-36 Pints
Berries (except Strawberries)	5-8 Cups	Jam	1 Quart	2-3 Pints
Blackberries	1 Quart	Jam	1 Pint	3/4 Quart
Blueberries	1 Quart/3 lbs.	Jam, Jelly	1 Pint	1 Quart
Cherries	1 Quart / 2-2 1/2 lbs.	Jelly	1 Quart Unpitted	1 Quart Unpitted
Grapes	1 Bushel	Juice	16	

			Quart	
Grapes	2 Quarts	Jelly	1 Quart	
Peaches	1 Bushel / 48 lbs.		18-24 Quarts	32-48 Pints
Peaches	2-2 1/2 lbs.			2 Pints
Pears	1 Bushel / 56 lbs.		20-25 Quarts	40-50 Pints
Pears	2-2 1/2 lbs.		1 Quart	2 Pints
Plums	1 Bushel		24-30 Quart	
Plums	2-2 1/2 lbs.		1 Quart	
Strawberries	24 Quart Crate		12-16 Quarts	38 Pints
Strawberries	6-8 Cups		1 Quart	2 Pints

Now that you know the basics let's take a look at the business aspect and just what goes into starting a homemade food business.

PICKLING

THERE are many varieties of pickled and fermented foods that are classified based on their ingredients and how they are prepared:

- ❖ Regular dill pickles and sauerkraut are fermented and cured for three weeks. Refrigerator dills are fermented for a week.

- ❖ Fresh-pack or quick-process pickles are not fermented, but some are brined for several hours or overnight then drained and covered in seasonings or vinegar.

- ❖ Fruit pickles are often prepared by heating fruit in a seasoned syrup and acidified with either vinegar or lemon juice.

- ❖ Relishes are made from chopped fruits and vegetables that are then cooked in vinegar and seasonings.

It is important to note that the level of acidity in a pickled product is vital to the taste, texture, and safety. Therefore, you shouldn't alter the vinegar, food or water proportions in a recipe or use any vinegar that doesn't have the known acidity.

It is a good idea only to follow recipes that have tested proportions of ingredients. A minimum, uniform level of acid is required to prevent the growth of botulinum bacteria in a mixed product.

SELECTING INGREDIENTS

For pickling, you want to use fresh, firm fruits or vegetables that don't have any spoilage. Carefully measure or weight all amounts since the appropriate proportion will determine flavor and safety.

You should only use canning or pickling salt. The noncaking material that is added to other types of salts will cloud the brine. Flake salt is also not recommended since it varies in density and isn't suitable for pickled and fermented foods.

Often white granulated and brown sugar are used. Unless a reliable recipe calls for corn syrup or honey, you should avoid these since they can cause undesirable flavors.

It is recommended to only use white distilled and cider vinegar of 5 percent acidity or fifty grain. White vinegar is best if you want a light color, as is usually the case with fruits and cauliflower.

REDUCED SALT CONTENT PICKLES

If you are interested in making pickles with less salt, then you should consult Guide 6 of the USDA Complete Guide to Home Canning.

When it comes to fresh-packed pickles, cucumbers acidify quickly with vinegar. These pickles can be safely prepared with reduced or no salt, but the quality may be lower in both texture and flavor. You should start out making small quantities first to make sure you like them.

When it comes to salt in fermented sauerkraut and brined pickles, the salt is what gives the characteristic flavor and is also key to the texture and safety of the overall product. Fermented foods rely on salt to grow desirable bacteria while preventing the growth of others. You should never try to make sauerkraut or fermented pickles by simply cutting back on salt.

FIRMING AGENTS

For fermented pickles, alum can be used safely to firm up the pickles. However, it isn't necessary and is often not included in tested recipes. Alum doesn't work to improve the firmness of quick-process pickles.

The calcium in lime will also enhance pickle firmness. You can use food-grade lime as a lime-water solution for soaking fresh cucumbers 12 to 24 hours before you pickle them. In order for the pickles to be safe, you'll need to remove the excess lime absorbed by the cucumbers. In order to do this, you'll need to drain the lime-water solution, rinse and then resoak the cucumbers in fresh water for one hour. Repeat this process two more times.

Another option for firming pickles is to process the cucumber for 30 minutes in water at 180 degrees Fahrenheit. This will also help to prevent spoilage, but only if the water temperature never drops below 180 degrees Fahrenheit.

PREVENTING SPOILAGE

Microorganisms cause the pickle products to be subject to spoilage. Yeasts, molds, and enzymes will affect flavor, color, and texture. You can prevent these problems by processing pickles in a boiling water canner.

CHOOSING CUCUMBERS

You will need about 14 pounds of cucumbers per load of 7 quarts. For a load of 9 pints, you will need about 9 pounds of cucumbers. You should choose firm cucumbers that are about 1 and 1/2 inches for gherkins and 4 inches for dills. For relishes, you can use odd-shaped and more mature cucumbers. These also work well for bread-and-butter style pickles.

LOW-TEMPERATURE PASTEURIZATION TREATMENT

For the best product texture, you should use this method for pickling, but you need to carefully manage it to avoid potential spoilage.

Place the jars in a canner filled half way with warm water, about 120 to 140 degrees Fahrenheit. Next, add hot water to a level about an inch above the jars. Heat the water enough to maintain 180 to 185 degrees Fahrenheit for 30 minutes.

Use a candy or jelly thermometer to make sure the temperature maintains appropriately throughout the entire 30 minutes. Temperatures over 185 degrees will cause the pickles to soften. Only use this method when a recipe calls for it, otherwise use regular canning methods.

Here is a Food Channel YouTube video on how to make Dill Pickle, take a look.

https://www.youtube.com/watch?v=e_vRu61oYho

PART- 2

THE BUSINESS

9 STEPS TO TAKING YOUR HOMEMADE FOOD BUSINESS TO THE NEXT LEVEL

ONCE you see your products are selling in local farmer's and Flea markets and you decide to take your business to the next stage (state, regional or even national), you will need to take few more steps.

1. Incorporate your business by filing the articles of incorporation to your local probate court
2. Apply and Obtain your EIN(Employer Identification Number) from IRS
3. Apply and obtain all local, city, county and state business and occupational licenses
4. Rent or build a commercial kitchen according to your Local Health Dept. guidelines
5. Obtain Food and Fire permits
6. But appropriate liability and other related insurance, We bought something that is called BOP(Business Owner's Policy)
7. Install a good bookkeeping system

8. Make Sure your labels are made according to USDA guidelines
9. Have a lab test your product to determine shelf life. (So you can put the Expiration date)

Though incorporating your business is a simple process, but it can be confusing to a newcomer as there are few things you will have to understand and clarify beforehand. Let's discuss these options.

BUSINESS STRUCTURE

When starting a business, there are five different business structures you can choose from:

- Sole Proprietor
- Partnership
- Corporation (Inc. or Ltd.)
- S Corporation
- Limited Liability Company (LLC)

SOLE PROPRIETOR

This is the most common structure for a cleaning business. It is used for a business owned by a single person or a married couple. Under this structure, the owner is personally liable for all business debts and may file on their personal income tax.

PARTNERSHIP

This is another inexpensive business structure to form. It often requires an agreement between two or more individuals who are going to jointly own and operate a business. The partners will share all aspects of the business in accordance with the agreement. Partnerships don't pay taxes, but they need to file an informational return. Individual partners then report their share of profits and losses on their personal tax returns.

CORPORATION (INC. OR LTD.)

This is one of the more complex business structures and has the most startup costs of any business structure. It isn't a very common structure among cleaning businesses since there are shares of stocks involved. Profits are taxed both at the corporate level and again when distributed to shareholders. When you structure a business at this level, there are often lawyers involved.

S CORPORATION

This is one of the most popular types of business entity people form to it avoid double taxation. It is taxed similarly to a partnership entity. But an S Corp. needs to be approved to be classified as such, so it isn't very common among cleaning businesses.

LIMITED LIABILITY COMPANY (LLC)

This is the second most common business structure among cleaning businesses. It offers benefits for small businesses since it reduces the risk of losing all your personal assets in case you are faced with a lawsuit. It provides a clear separation between business and personal assets. You can also elect to be taxed as a corporation, which saves you money come tax time.

If you are unsure which specific business structure you should choose then, you can discuss it with an accountant. They will direct you in the best possible option for what your business goals are.

HOW AND WHERE TO SELL YOUR PRODUCTS

ONCE you have decided to expand your food business into a commercial kitchen, then you have multiple options of where to sell your products. According to cottage laws (I explained this law in the Legal section of this book), without appropriate legal steps, you will only be able to sell at local farmers and Flea markets. After conforming to the legal requirements, you can sell to a number of other sources as well.

You can't expect to sell jam, jellies and make a profit unless people know that your line of products exist. There are many ways you can choose to promote your products, and you don't need to use all of them. Rather you want to choose the best methods that will make people aware of your jams and be the friendliest option for your business budget. Let's take a look at your options

ONLINE

In today's electronic focused society, perhaps the best option is to have an online presence. Having a website will allow you to appear on search engines and get attention from potential customers around the world who otherwise may not get a chance to find out about your jams and jelly.

If you are going to set up an online presence, the first thing you need to do is find a web host and create an account. For more professionalism, you should consider purchasing your own domain name if you can afford it before building your website. Remember I said you do need to come up with a name for your brand, and I also suggested that you should buy the domain name of that brand so if your business takes off, you can have a full blown online business and establish your brand name on the world wide web.

It only cost around $10-$12/year to buy a domain name. You can buy domain names from www.Name.com, www.godaddy.com, www.Register.com or any other online domain registrar. You can always purchase the domain name and open your online store later, buying a domain does not force you to open an online retail store.

Even without HTML knowledge, you can still build a decent website with the templates most web hosts offer, or you can hire a freelancer designer to put one together for you. We hired our web designer from www.upwork.com, and it cost us around $650 to get the site up and running.

Once you have your website up, you should make sure you provide information on the products you offer and include a portfolio of your jam, jelly, pickles and any other related products that you make so people can get a good idea of what you have to offer. Then you'll be ready to set up for accepting online sales.

AN ONLINE STORE

With websites such as eBay and Etsy, it is easier than ever to sell homemade jam, jelly, and pickles online. However, many of these options will deduct a percentage of the total sales so you may have to set your prices accordingly. Another option is to set up an online store on your website and sell directly to customers. One big downside to this is to let customers know that your site exists. For that, you may have to spend a lot of money on online advertising with Google PPC (Pay per Click), and other social media ads.

A MAILING LIST

Once you have a website and start developing an online presence, you may want to consider starting a mailing list. This is a great way to get repeat customers since interested individuals can sign up for a mailing list. About once a month you can send out a newsletter showing your newest products and potentially a special discount to increase the incentive to purchase.

NETWORKING SITES

Customers want a way to contact sellers directly as well as a place where they can publicly express their shopping experiences. If you provide this, you will not only draw attention to your business, but you can also potentially increase sales. Keep in contact with your customers through networking sites such as Facebook and Twitter. Just remember to always include a link back to your website so people can find you easily.

PPC ADVERTISING

If simply having your items listed for sale online isn't doing enough, you can consider increasing some attention by buying PPC or pay per click advertising. You can do this through Google or other search engines. As it sounds, this type of advertising means you only pay when someone actually comes to your website through a PPC link. You can often determine how much you pay and set a daily limit. This option isn't for everyone, but it is another online advertising option.

OFFLINE

Just because we live in an electronic and connected society, doesn't mean offline methods are no longer effective. Sometimes the best sales come from local areas and not worldwide sales. So be sure also to consider some offline methods of promotion to get your products noticed.

BRANDING AND IDENTITY

Have some nice business cards printed that you can include with each purchase or simply to give to people you meet. This can be an excellent way to get both new and repeat sales. It may be a good idea to have a nice logo designed to increase your promotions and have things look more professional.

You can go to your local Office Depot, Office Max or online stores like VistaPrints.com and get 500 business cards printed for less than $20, make sure to ask for their special coupon pricing.

LOCAL PAPERS AND FLIERS

If you can afford it, consider taking out an ad in the local newspaper. Another option that can be a little cheaper is to print some fliers and then post them around town in heavily frequented areas such as the local coffee shop. Anything you print should include your contact information and the URL for your online store. If you are hanging fliers in a business, be sure to get the manager's approval before posting.

COMMUNITY EVENTS

The best way to get local exposure is to sponsor events within the community. Offer to supply Free Jam, Jelly or Pickles for events in exchange for a mention. This is a great place to start for a small candle making business. Works best for many Church and other local similar community events.

INTRODUCTORY OFFERS

Your homemade Jams and Jellies maybe the yummiest jams that are out in the market, but how would the customers know that? You need to give people a reason to choose yours over others. Competitive pricing is one option (I don't recommend it), but you can also offer special deals.

Give a discount to first-time customers, holiday specials or clearance events for older stock. This way you get people interested, and you don't have to affect your profits long term by lowering your prices.

These are just some of the main options for promoting your jams and jelly. The methods of promotion are limited only by your imagination.

SELLING PRODUCTS TO GIFT SHOPS

One excellent way to both make a profit for your jam and jelly-making business while also increase your promotion is to sell them to gift shops. In addition to gift shops, you can also include small boutiques and consignment stores they may specialize in local craft goods and exotic foods or one-of-a-kind gift options. Other options include local specialty food stores.

RESEARCH POTENTIAL STORES

Before you approach any store make sure you do your research to ensure you are targeting the right locations and setting the right price point. Gift shops will often specialize in certain products, so you want to choose one that features merchandise that compliments your products rather than detracts from them. You also want to make sure that you are choosing gift shops with price points similar to what you expect to get for your jams.

CHOOSING CONSIGNMENT OR WHOLESALE

Some gift shops will be open to buying your products wholesale or at a reduced rate so they can resell them for a profit, but others are going to only offer a consignment option. When you are offered a consignment option, it means you will be allowed to display your products for sale, and the shop owner will get a percentage of your sales. It is up to you to determine which option is best for you based on the cost and earnings perspective of your products. Then you can limit your focus to gift shops that will work with the option you're looking for.

HAVE A PROPOSAL

Before approaching gift shops, farmer's market or any food stores make sure you have prepared a sales proposal. A great proposal is one that includes an overview of your entire product line including how they are made, what ingredients you use and the sizes, shapes, and flavors you carry.

Provide a description of how your jams and jellies are different from others. Have a breakdown of price points for each size and outline how much inventory you have on hand or how quickly you can produce new jams and jellies. You should have some product samples and ask to meet with the shop owner or purchasing manager to discuss your product.

PITCH YOUR PROPOSAL

If possible, you want to visit potential new customers in personal so potential buyers can meet you. If you want to expand regionally then consider an eye-catching sales brochure with professional photos of your candles and have a website ready to show what you have to offer. Before spreading out be sure to do your research on a larger scale and find gift shops, farmer's market or other food stores that meet your criteria in areas you are looking to expand. Offer to send samples and sales materials, so the store has a chance to get a first-hand look at what you have to offer.

GO TO TRADE SHOWS

Another good option is to consider setting up a vendor booth at a trade show. This can help provide you with exposure and allow you to meet with buyers from different retail outlets. If you can't afford a both, you can at least attend a trade show and participate in networking events. This can help you develop new contacts that can eventually develop into new sales.

One thing that is sure to come up at some point is selling wholesale. Whether you are selling large amounts to a single store or you get a larger contract to sell to a major retailer; you may eventually be asked to wholesale. Let's consider how you can do this to have the best potential outcome for your business.

SELLING WHOLESALE

Before you get asked to sell your line of products wholesale it is important that you do some research on the wholesale jelly market. You can choose to sell wholesale directly to a buyer or through a wholesale distributor on a commission basis. When you work with a distributor, they will attend trade shows and make sales calls on your behalf so you can focus more of your time on the important part of making candles and efficiently running your company.

Start your research by considering the competition in retail stores. Take note of the price, shape, type and size of the competitions jams and jellies. Determine what makes yours unique. Perhaps you use only organic ingredients or your jams, or that it is all natural and you use no artificial colorings or flavorings. There are a number of things that can make your jams stand out from the competition.

When it comes to pricing your jams for wholesale you want to price them at half retail price. Stores will often mark up their inventory by 100 percent over cost. For example, if you sell wholesale at $4 a jar, the retail store will likely charge $8 a jar.

It is important to consider exactly what it costs to produce your Jams. You don't want the cost of making a jar to exceed 50 percent of your wholesale price. If it goes over 50 percent, then you need to either adjust your wholesale price higher or determine ways you can decrease production cost.

Once you have a good idea of the appropriate wholesale price, you know what to quote a potential buyer.

PRICING YOUR PRODUCTS

PRICING and marketing homemade food can be a challenging process since there are many variables to be considered. You can even set a price for your product based on the value that is provided to customers. One important factor to take into consideration when pricing your products is what your customers like, need and their willingness to pay for a specific product.

A product needs to provide a solution for the customer. You want to provide a product that is more than simply food since most local foods are going to be higher priced than the same products mass produced and sold in grocery stores.

While calculating the costs and returns can seem a daunting and tedious task, it provides you with the peace of mind that you are receiving adequate income for all your work. The price you charge needs to cover your production costs as well as your desired net income for the business. A lot of small businesses neglect this step, which can lead to a loss of money over time. Simply taking the time to calculate costs will ensure you make income from your food and not lose any money.

Consider the Following Example:

Cost for 8 pints jam/jelly ingredients = $7.00

Cost for 8 pint jars and lids = $5.00

Cost for labor at 30 minutes x $12.00/hour = $6.00

Total Cost = $7.00 + $5.00 + $6.00 = $18.00

Divided by 8 jars = $2.25

Transportation: 40 miles roundtrip to market x $0.60/mile = $24.00

Marketing and Selling Labor: 20 minutes social media and 3 hours at market x $12.00 = $38.40

Total Cost of Selling at a Local Market: $24.00 + $38.40 = $62.40

Market cost is divided by the number of jars: $62.40/8 = $7.80

You sell an average of 16 pints of jam at the local market: $7.80/16 = $0.48 per jar.

Market cost $0.48 + cost of goods per container $2.25 = $2.73 per pint.

Add 50% additional costs such as damaged and unsold products, kitchen costs, advertising, etc. = $1.36

$2.73 + $1.36 = $4.09

Stall space fees at the local market are 5% of sales: 5% of $2.73 = $0.13

The price charged per container will need to be at least $2.86 + $1.36 = $4.22 a pint

If you use a similar calculation, it will help you to determine which foods will provide you with an income and keep the production costs within a range the customers are willing to spend. Sometimes local foods may cost more to produce than a customer is willing to pay. This is where marketing comes in handy.

You need to know where to position your product and what price to offer to reach targeted customers. To sell to targeted customers, they need to know enough about your product to want to buy them. When planning costs you want to include costs associated with gaining access to customers. When you know your customer's habits, you'll be better able to determine how to access them. This is also known as customer acquisition cost.

The key is to connect with your customers. Those who are interested in local food want to know the story behind a product, such as the person who produced it and how it can meet their needs. Customers can easily get cheap items at the larger stores. Customers want to be educated on what can solve their problem.

If a customer feels connected to a product, they are willing to pay more. You also want to focus on making food that is unique and of exceptionally high quality. This is what establishing your brand with some kind of uniqueness is vital.

MARKETING & PROMOTING YOUR NEW BUSINESS

MARKETING TIPS FOR RETAIL STORES

WHEN it comes to selling in retail stores, you need to focus on creating a product that is both safe and appealing. A customer is going to have many options at a retail store, and you need to make your food stand out from others and get people to purchase. Let's look at what marketing you can use to make your product stand out from the competition.

PACKAGING

This is often the decisive factor for customers when making a purchasing decision. You not only want packaging that keeps your food fresh, but it also needs to tempt people to purchase. When it comes to jams, jellies and pickles; if your product is already visually appealing, then you may want to consider clear packaging materials in order to showcase the natural color of your product. You'll also want to make sure your products are properly labeled according to legal standards.

SHELF LIFE

Nearly all food products are perishable at some point. When selling to a retail store you need to have a clear idea of how long your product will last. Your marketing and distribution should be based on your shelf life information.

WHOLESALE MARKETING

To sell in a retail store, you also need to convince the manager to carry your product. You should research stores in your local area and determine which ones sell to a target market most likely to want your product. Visit or call these stores to ask about their policies for new products. You should have a marketing package prepared that includes samples and product information such as a delivery schedule, shelf life, and product price information.

RETAIL MARKETING

Even after you convince a store manager to carry your product, you still need to market to shoppers and encourage them to purchase. You can offer introductory discounts, design small signs for grocery shelves or schedule product demonstrations and samples. The best thing you can do is put a face to the product and communicate clearly the selling points of your food.

MARKETING TIPS FOR LOCAL MARKETS

People are being drawn to quality, homemade goods and if you have a passion for cooking, you can sell your goods at the local farmers market and craft sales. Let's look at how you can sell your jams, jellies, and pickles at a local market and have a profitable business.

FLAVORS

When you first start out, you should stick with established recipes then use your experiences and those of your customers to branch out into other flavors. If possible consider adding some unique and local flavors that will attract people and give you something the competition doesn't have. You should also set out an array of flavors and allow potential customers to try samples. This can not only lead to new sales but will allow you to get feedback on flavors so you know where to focus your efforts.

STAY SMALL

Things taste different when made in small batches rather than large and commercially processed batches. When you make things in large batches, you end up changing the chemistry. Therefore, it is best to make your jams, jellies, and pickles in small batches. You'll need to carefully plan out your supply purchases and your cooking schedules, but small batches also mean you aren't going to waste anything if it doesn't sell fast.

Also, most jams and jellies reach their peak flavor within days of being sealed in jars. If you prepare too many in advance, people aren't going to be able to enjoy these flavors if your jars sit around for a while before getting sold. It will also allow you to preserve the brightness and color of your food. Food that looks and tastes better is the key to repeat customers and profitable business.

PART – 3

LEGAL & SAFETY REQUIREMENTS

LEGAL REQUIREMENTS

WHEN it comes to selling homemade food, there are a lot of legal aspects you need to consider. Before you start making your first batch of food to sell, consider the following legal points you need to meet.

FEDERAL FOOD AND DRUG ADMINISTRATION (FDA) REGULATIONS

No matter what type of food you want to sell, the first thing you need to do is make sure you are in compliance with federal laws. The FDA has a number of regulations regarding the production, packaging, labeling and distribution of homemade food. It is a good idea to look through an FDA compliance manual. These manuals are especially important if you are going to make your food at home and not in a commercial factory.

STATE AND LOCAL LAWS

In addition to federal laws, you also want to make sure your business is in compliance with state and local laws as well. It can be a bit challenging to determine what laws apply to your home business, but if you want to stay in business, you need to make sure you get them right. The main requirements to learn about are those regarding licensing as well as health and safety requirements.

BUSINESS LICENSING

It is a good idea to incorporate your business before you start selling homemade food. This will protect you from being personally liable for lawsuits that are filed against you. When selling food, legal action is always a possibility. For most small businesses the best option is to become an LLC or a privately held corporation. Take the time to read up on your options and determine what is right for you.

BUSINESS INSURANCE

It is also important that you have your business properly insured before you start selling homemade food. As with all business ventures, insurance gives you a financial safety net in the event that the worst case scenario happens. There are a number of insurance companies that provide specific policies for people running a food business, so take the time to look around and find the best deal.

LEGAL ADVICE

Since there are so many legal areas involved in starting a food business, it can be a good idea to seek legal advice. If you are confused or overwhelmed by all the rules and laws that affect you then consider consulting with a lawyer before getting your business started.

MEETING THE LEGAL REQUIREMENTS

IF YOU want to sell your homemade jams, jellies, and pickles beyond the local farmers market, then you are going to have to take several things into consideration. Before you can sell out of state, to stores or to distributors, you need to meet several requirements. Each individual situation will be based on specific products, and you can get the specific information you need through your local health department. When you want to expand your business, you'll need to consider the following.

LOCAL HEALTH DEPARTMENT ISSUES

Talk to the individual in your area that addresses processed foods, and they can tell you what is required for you to produce and sell your food. Just remember every local health department is different when it comes to specific requirements, so it is best to talk to your local county health department and get a list of requirements that you need to comply to obtain a food permit and produce food commercially for resale.

USE A COMMERCIAL KITCHEN FOR FOOD PREPARATION

Commercial food products need to be processed in an inspected kitchen that is certified by the local health inspector. Before you try to remodel your home kitchen (a bad idea), you should consider renting a commercial kitchen to get the experience and determine what equipment you need. In some large cities, you may be able to rent community kitchens by the hour. In smaller cities, you may be able to rent a certified kitchen at a senior center, school facility or restaurant.

Make sure the kitchen is able to be approved for processing your food by talking with the local health inspector. If you can't rent a certified kitchen, you can consider outsourcing to a co-packer. This is a company who is willing to produce your product for you. It is best to choose a co-packer who has the capability and experience to manufacture your product.

After starting out at home, when the demand for our product grew, we made a deal with one of our local church community center where they agreed to rent their commercial kitchen to us four days a week excluding weekends for a very reasonable price. So if you look around you should be able to find a commercial kitchen that complies with all your local food safety laws, all you do is bring your own canners, jars, and ingredients and start making jams, jellies and pickles in batches.

FOOD SAFETY TRAINING

At least one individual in the kitchen at all times needs to have a food safety training through SafeServe. You can get information on local classes from the local health agency.

It is generally a 6-hour one-day training course, once you get this done, it is good for a few years.

APPROVED RECIPES AND PROCEDURES

Some states will require you to have your recipes and processing procedures approved by a processing authority. These provide product testing to determine whether or not the process you use is safe. Processing authorities keep up-to-date records on national food safety regulations so they can make sure products fulfill all standards. Contact your local county and city health inspector or search online to see if there is a processing authority in your area and whether or not you need their approval. We didn't have to do that in our state but thought I should mention it just in case.

An appropriate processing authority needs to a recognized independent lab that has the expertise needed to run the tests required to show a food products safety including pH, water availability and microbial analysis. They also need to provide you with written reports that validate your process or results.

FOOD SAFETY PROCEDURES PLAN, CRITICAL CONTROL POINTS, AND STANDARD OPERATING PROCEDURES

You need to have a production plan that shows the procedures followed during every production process that keeps a product safe. Critical control points (CCP) are the critical procedures that prevent microbial growth. This would include boiling in the water bath for the appropriate length of time. You also want to outline the standard cleaning and hygiene procedures for workers and surfaces within the production facility.

The Hazard Analysis and Critical Control Points plan need to include the food safety procedure, the recipes and the tracking of products. The processing authority can help you develop this plan.

Each food product you make should have a detailed paper trail for each ingredient. A document should outline the in-house handling of ingredients that including the date they enter the kitchen, how they are cared for, the way they are processed, how they are packaged, how they are cared for after processing, and how they are labeled.

You also want a separate detailed paper trail for the distribution of products to customers. These details allow tracking the origin of tainted ingredients so customers can be alerted.

REGISTER WITH THE STATE HEALTH AUTHORITY

Approved recipes from the processing authority, product plans and documentation and proposed product labels all need to be submitted to the State Health Authority. You should talk to the local health department about your product to understand what you need to consider.

Each state has different registration procedures and costs based on the food products and the specific food safety situation. Once you submit your application, the health department will send back a formal response that tells you which areas need to be addressed in order to get approved.

Discuss and reply with the changes needed. You can always contact the health department for clarity. The health department is there to help you have a successful and safe business.

FEDERAL APPROVALS

Lastly, the local health department can help you with identifying what federal approvals you need for your product. For a high-acid or acidified food that has a pH below 4.6, you will need approval from the Food and Drug Administration (FDA) and the appropriate applications. Low-acid canned products are going to require more regulation and will likely require a co-packer facility.

Another aspect of being legal when selling your homemade food is following labeling requirements.

COTTAGE FOOD LAWS

WITHIN each state, the cottage food law is the legal permission or ban on the selling of homemade food. In the last few years, states have either tightened or loosened these laws. There are plenty of farmers markets and local craft fairs where individuals with little to no funding can start a small business idea and bring in extra money. At these events, the booths selling homemade food often draw the most attention from customers.

At one time the process of making and selling homemade goods was easy. Now with modern cottage food laws, it can be difficult, if not entirely illegal, to sell homemade food. If you are planning to sell your homemade food you want to take the time to learn about cottage food laws and how they affect you.

WHAT IS THE COTTAGE FOOD LAW

Cottage food is considered bread, pickles, candy, syrups, jams, jellies and pretty much any other items that people craft in the kitchen. The cottage part refers to an individual operation that is too small to afford the necessary licensing.

Cottage food laws define how you can sell homemade food for profit. The rules apply to any low-risk foods or those that don't have a high risk of botulism or listeria. Foods at a greater risk for these toxins need to follow very strict licensing and legal procedures.

WHY THE LAWS EXIST

Public health is a major concern. That is why local health departments do surprise inspections at restaurants; to make sure the customers aren't getting poisoned. These departments have controls over the type of appliances used to cook, specific times and temperatures, and overall cleanliness of all parts to the restaurants including kitchen, bathrooms and dining areas. There is no such supervision when it comes to home kitchens. When it comes to canned foods, any slight variation can cause illness and problems.

On the other hand, if local health codes applied to all kitchens then those selling homemade goods wouldn't have a chance. The cost of inspections and food handling licenses would take all the money that selling of goods would generate. Cottage food laws were designed to give small food producers a chance. They don't give complete freedom to make and sell all types of homemade food, but it at least makes it possible to sell something.

WHAT AND WHERE YOU CAN SELL

Selling homemade food isn't legal in all states. For example, in New Jersey, it is illegal to sell any type of homemade food. On the other hand, in Idaho, there are no cottage food laws, so the rules vary based on the specific health districts to determine what is and aren't allowed. Wisconsin is like most states; you are allowed to sell only at local events and farmers markets. Depending on where you are, you should find out if the cottage law applies to you or not.

When an item is sold under cottage food laws, they are exempt from local codes and licensing. This means that only certain sales are legal. Safety is the main indication of what is allow under the cottage food law. If food is susceptible to botulism, then they are illegal in pretty much all the states. The more acceptable foods are jams, jellies, pickles and baked goods. Although again, the specific rules can vary by states.

Often meat isn't allowed since there are widespread health concerns. In order for farmers to sell meat to the public, they need to have it USDA-inspected or offer is through a program where consumers buy animals and then pay to have them butchered. Some foods like cheeses and milk are banned if they come from raw milk. Even dairy products that are made from store bought milk require special licensing.

Fruits and vegetables grown in a garden don't require any special licensing as long as they aren't cut or altered. Some states allow home grown produce to be sold as cottage food and others don't. As such, some states allow canned food and others don't.

You can look up your own state's cottage food laws or health code to determine what is and isn't allowed in your state. Most health department sites will give you details on where selling is allowed and what types of food you can sell. They will also have a set maximum revenue that you can make in a year. The health department will also let you know how a label needs to be written, whether or not you can sell across state lines and if there is a maximum sales or profit.

Now you know the legal background for why you have to jump through so many legal hoops to sell your homemade food. Most of these rules have to do with the safety and health of your food. Let's consider the major food and workplace safety issues you need to consider in order to be in compliance with a lot of the legal regulations.

LABELING REQUIREMENTS

INDIVIDUALS are allowed to make jams, jellies, and pickles in their home kitchens and sell them as long as they meet certain conditions regarding the labeling, who makes and sells them and where they are sold. Jams, jellies, and pickles made in a home kitchen need to be sold by the manufacturer directly to the consumer. This doesn't include taking an order and shipping to the customer. I'll discuss more about the sale requirements and aspect later. For now, let's look at the labeling requirements.

WHAT TO INCLUDE

Jams, jellies, and pickles made in a home kitchen and sold at a local market need to have the following on the label:

- ✓ Name and address of the person making the product.
- ✓ Common name of the food.
- ✓ Name of all ingredients.

- ✓ Net weight of the product in metric and English units.

- ✓ A statement that the product hasn't been inspected by the local or federal government. See your local regulations for the specific wording that needs to be included.

- ✓ Everything on the label needs to be in English.

SPECIAL LABELING REQUIREMENTS

One exemption to the food code is the home production of "sugar-free" or "no sugar added" jams and jellies. Regular jams and jellies rely on sugar used and the finished pH of the product to prevent harmful bacteria.

The pH scale measures that acidity of food products. Less sugar can potentially allow moisture for harmful bacteria to grow. This means the pH becomes the only barrier to harmful bacterial growth. For example, if a fruit has a pH over 4.0 and artificial sweeteners are added then botulism can become a problem.

Extra steps are needed to ensure the safety of products that rely on acidity to prevent harmful bacteria from posing a problem. The two main steps include the following:

1. Products containing artificial sweeteners need to have a lab test the ph.

2. Jam or jelly with a pH under 4.0 can be made in a home kitchen under the statutory exemption in most states.

However, the manufacturing process needs to be strictly followed to produce a product that has the same pH as the tested sample. Even a slight change to your recipe will require a re-test.

If a product is made from fruits and contains natural sugars, then the label needs to state "No Sugar Added" since it contains natural sugars from the fruit after processing. Sugar-free or no sugar added jam or jelly needs to have a pH between 4.0 and 4.6 in an inspected or regulated facility.

The pH needs to be tested on each batch with a quality pH meter and a clear record of the results. Sugar-free or no sugar added jam or jelly with a pH over 4.6 isn't allow to be produced in a home kitchen under any circumstances. These products are deemed low acid food, and the manufacturer needs to attend a Better Process Control School and have the product evaluated by an authority in accordance with federal law.

Jams or jellies made with juices also require testing. If the pH is under 4.0, then the pH is deemed the primary control point, and the producer can continue. If the pH is over 4.0, then water activity becomes the main control point, and the water activity needs to be tested in a laboratory.

If the water activity is below 0.80, the jam or jelly can be made under the food code exemption in most states. The recipe and process cannot be changed, or the pH and water activity measurements are no longer valid and require retesting. If the water activity is between 0.80 and 0.85, then the product needs to be made in a regulated facility and the water activity closely monitored. Any product that has a water activity over 0.85 is considered a low acid or acidified food, which is not allowed to be made in a home kitchen.

To make these products, you would need to attend a Better Process Control School and have the product tested by a process authority.

Now that you have all the paperwork figured out, you're ready to start selling your homemade food. With all of the legal paperwork in place, you are going to have lots more places to sell your food.

FOOD AND WORKPLACE SAFETY

ALL RESTAURANTS and food manufacturers need to follow food safety regulations, and you as a homemade food producer are no exception. You need to consider both food safety practices and workplace safety issues. The importance of food safety shouldn't be understated, and you want to carefully consider them. Food safety procedures prevent the spread of foodborne illnesses, protecting both you and your customers.

BASIC SANITATION AND SAFETY

Food preparation, packaging, and handling should be done in a separate place from other domestic activities such as family meal preparation, dish washing, clothes washing, kitchen cleaning or guest entertainment. When working with food, you should follow four basic guidelines:

1. Don't allow smoking during food operations.

2. Don't allow anyone with a contagious illness to work with food while ill.

3. Wash hands and exposed arm portions before preparing or packaging food.

4. Minimize any bare hand contact of food by using utensils, single-use gloves or bakery papers; especially when you are packaging ready-to-eat foods.

All equipment and utensils involved in the process of making homemade food should be kept in clean and operable condition. There are three guideline rules to follow when it comes to your utensils and equipment:

1. Before each use, you should wash, rinse and sanitize all food contact surfaces, equipment, and utensils.

2. Make sure any water that comes into contact with food products meets clean drinking water standards.

3. All food preparation and equipment storage areas need to be free of insects and rodents.

All food that is used for manufacturing, producing, preparation, packaging, storage or transportation should be kept free from spoilage and adulteration. You can do this by observing the following four guidelines:

1. Purchase ingredients from approved sources.

2. Protect food from dirt, rodents, unnecessary handling, droplet contamination, overhead leakage or other environmental contamination.

3. Prevent any cross contamination of foods or ingredients with any raw animal products or chemicals.

4. All food should be prepackaged in order to protect it from contamination during transportation, display, sale and purchase.

WHERE TO GET FOOD

You should only purchase your produce and other ingredients from approved sources. This would include licensed farms with a producer's certificate, commercial growers or commercial food suppliers. You should always know where your food ingredients come from and whether or not the supplier follows proper food safety protocol. A licensed supplies need to maintain their license by complying with state and federal regulations.

These processes ensure safe food products. Most food product recalls are the result of ingredient contamination, missed labeling of allergen ingredients or contamination from pathogens or debris. When you track the ingredients, you use you will be able to know whether or not your product contains dangerous recalled ingredients or if your product is safe to consume.

In most cities, there are commercial farmer's markets this is where most restaurant owners and other food retailers go to get their fruits and veggies. You can also find a few suppliers that deliver what you order every week. At first, I just made trips to these markets and bought what I needed, but as our business grew, I had them deliver which saved time and energy.

SELECTION, STORAGE, AND PREPARATION OF INGREDIENTS

Food safety also relies on the proper selection, storage, and preparation of ingredients. You should choose ingredients that are in sound condition and regularly check for spoilage, contamination or adulteration.

Any ingredients that require refrigeration should be stored promptly. Any leftover cut produce should be discarded if it is left at room temperature for longer than two hours.

Any dry ingredients such as your pectin and sweeteners should be stored in air-tight containers in a cool and dry location. This will prevent spoilage and weevil infestation. Weevils are small beetles that infest grain and rice foods. They have the ability to chew through paper or plastic packaging. If you notice any signs of weevils and/or their eggs you shouldn't use the products in food production.

Before using any fruits and vegetables, you should wash them with cool tap water. Even if you are going to peel them, you want to wash them to prevent dirt and bacteria from getting transferred to the peeler or knife and then onto the fruit or vegetable. Dry produce with a clean cloth or paper towel to reduce any present bacteria.

If you do your shopping with reusable grocery bags, you should regularly clean them. Canvas and cloth bags can be washed in the washing machine. Plastic reusable bags should be washed with hot, soapy water.

SHELF LIFE OF INGREDIENTS

Most food products have a date stamped on their packaging. These dates aren't required by the federal government, but they are useful to consumers. There are three types of dates you need to know:

1. A Sell-By date tells you how long a store can display products for sale. Products need to be purchased before the date expires.

2. A Best if used by or before date is one that serves as a recommendation for the best quality and flavor. This isn't an indication of food safety.

3. A Use By date is the last possible date for recommended product use at peak quality. This date is determined by the manufacturer and often refers to the best quality and not the product safety.

These dates don't always relate to the product use after purchase and home storage, with the exception of the Use By date. If other dates expire while you have it stored at home, then they should be safe and of good quality to use as long as they are handled properly.

Foods will often develop an odd odor, appearance or flavor as a result of bacteria spoilage. If you notice these characteristics, you shouldn't use that product. Mishandled food has an increased chance of bacteria and pathogens that could result in food-borne illness before or after the package date.

This would include food left unrefrigerated longer than two hours or being handled by someone who doesn't follow proper sanitation practices. To ensure safety and quality, you always want to follow handling and preparation instructions on the product label.

USE OF FROZEN FOODS

If you are going to be using frozen fruits or vegetables, then you should be aware of a few specific safety precautions. As soon as frozen foods start to thaw and become warmer than 41 degrees Fahrenheit, any bacteria present before freezing will start to multiply. Frozen foods should always be kept frozen until they are ready to be thawed and used.

The USDA offers three recommended ways to thaw foods safely:

1. In the refrigerator.

2. In cold water in a leak-proof bag and changing the water every 30 minutes.

3. In the microwave.

You should never thaw frozen foods on a counter.

WORKPLACE PREPARATION

Food safety goes beyond the food. You also need to consider proper cleaning of the kitchen and utensils before you prepare foods. Having a clean workplace is essential to preventing the spread of foodborne illness and contaminants. All kitchen surfaces such as countertops, utensils, cutting boards and appliances need to be cleaned with hot, soapy water. You can use natural cleansers to avoid sensitivities to chemicals like bleach; although bleach is often recommended for disinfecting surfaces.

You should also immediately clean counters if there is a drip or spill of any animal products such as raw egg, or blood from raw meat. Never use dirty or smelly dishcloths, towels or sponges since this can be a sign of bacterial growth. Dishcloths and towels should often be washed and in the hot cycle. Frequently wash hot pads. Utensils should be cleaned in hot, soapy water or run through the hot wash setting of the dishwasher.

You should have a cutting board specifically for produce to prevent cross-contamination of raw meats with fresh produce. Always use a clean cutting board and after use wash thoroughly in hot soapy water. You can also wash a cutting board in the dishwasher. Proper disinfection of a cutting board involves a fresh solution of one tablespoon of unscented, liquid chlorine bleach per gallon of water. Flood the surface with the bleach solution and allow it to stand for several minutes. Rinse with water and then allow to air dry.

If you are going to use bleach as a cleaning and disinfecting agent, then you should make sure you check the percentage. The bleach should be five percent sodium hypochlorite. Some generic brands may sell bleach with lower percentages.

PRODUCT TRACKING

In addition to proper cleaning, it is important to keep track of your source ingredients. This will allow you to know where sources of contamination come from should there be a complaint about a food product. It is a good idea to have a simple record system to record the ingredients you use and their sources.

Commercial operations need to have detailed documentation and records for all products produced and sold. In order to follow most state and federal regulations, the records need to detail how, where and when of each products' safety practices. While these records aren't required for a homemade food producer, it is a good idea to know what is required of commercial food producers so you can better understand what is needed to keep your consumers safe.

You can keep simple records that details out where you source each ingredient, create batch numbers for products produced and record your food safety practices this way you can identify the possible source of contamination if they occur or simply reassure your clients that you have taken the necessary steps to ensure a high-quality and safe product.

HAND WASHING

This is an important and vital aspect of food safety. The following steps are useful hand washing practices:

1. Rinse hands under running water.

2. Apply soap.

3. Rub hands vigorously for 10 to 15 seconds.

4. Remove dirt from under fingernails, the surface of hands and exposed areas of arms.

5. Rinse hands under running water.

6. Dry hands with a clean towel or single-use disposable paper towels.

7. Use a towel to turn off the faucet.

You should wash your hand before you prepare or handle food and after any of the following:

- Preparing food
- Touch raw food
- Switching food preparation tasks
- Touching eggs
- Using the restroom
- Coughing or sneezing
- Handling dirty dishes or garbage
- Petting animals
- Smoking
- Using the phone

- Touching hair, face, body or other people
- Touching a sore or cut

Now we are ready to look into the legal aspect of things. Let's first consider all the legal items you need to officially sell your homemade food.

LAST WORDS

HOPEFULLY, in this book, I was able to give you a good general overview of making jam, jelly, pickles and starting your own business. Now get out there and start making some money. And be successful, remember we only live once, so why not try best you can be and see where that may take you.

I wanted to thank you for buying my book; I am neither a professional writer nor an author, but rather a person who always had the passion for making homemade jams, jellies and such. In this book, I wanted to share my knowledge with you, as I know there are many people who share the same passion and drive as I do. So, this book is entirely dedicated to you.

Despite my best effort to make this book error free, if you happen to find any errors, I want to ask for your forgiveness ahead of time.

Just remember, my writing skills may not be best, but the knowledge I share here is pure and honest.

If you thought I added some value and shared some valuable information that you can use, please take a minute and post a review on wherever you bought this book from. This will mean the world to me. Thank you so much!!

Lastly, I wanted to thank my husband Bill and my daughters Jennifer, Jessica, and Janice for all their help and support throughout this book, without them, this book would not have been possible.

If you need to get in touch with me for any reason, please feel free to email me at valenciapublishing@gmail.com

GLOSSARY

Acid Foods - Foods that contain enough acid to have a pH of 4.6 or lower. This includes all fruits except figs, most tomatoes, fermented and pickled vegetables, relishes, jams, jellies, and marmalades. Acid foods can be processed in boiling water.

Ascorbic Acid - The chemical name of Vitamin C. Lemon juice contains large amounts of ascorbic acid and is often used to prevent peeled, light colored fruits and vegetables from browning. It can also be known by the term citric acid.

Bacteria - A large group of one-celled microorganism that is widely distributed in nature.

Blanching - Fruits and vegetables have a chemical compound in them known as enzymes. These enzymes are responsible for the loss of color, nutrients, and flavor when the fruits or vegetables are frozen or canned. You need to inactivate these enzymes to prevent the reaction from occurring.

This is done through the blanching process. This is done by exposing vegetables to boiling water or steam for a brief period of time, about two to five minutes. To prevent cooking, you need to drain off the hot water and rapidly cool in ice water. If you want top quality frozen vegetables then blanching is very essential. Blanching will also kill any microorganisms on the vegetable surface.

Blancher - A six to eight-quart lidded pot fitted with a perforated basket to hold food in boiling water or fitted with a rack to steam foods.

Boiling Water Canner - A large, standard-sized kettle with a jar rack for heat processing seven quarts or eight to nine pints in boiling water.

Botulism - An illness that results from eating a toxin produced by the growth of Clostridium Botulinum bacteria. Occurs often in moist, low-acid food that has less than two percent oxygen and stored between 40-120 degrees Fahrenheit. The bacteria is destroyed by proper heat processing. Freezer temperatures can inhibit the growth. In dried food, the growth is controlled by the low moisture controls. For fresh food, the growth is controlled by high oxygen.

Canners - Using an evenly heated environment in cooking vessels to subject canned goods to a temperature high enough to kill bacteria. The two approved methods are water bath canners and pressure canners.

Canning - The food preservation method that involves airtight, vacuum-sealed containers and heat processing in order to store food at normal home temperatures.

Canning Salt - Also known as pickling salt. This is regular table salt without iodine or anti-caking additives.

Citric Acid - A type of acid that can be added to canned foods. It will increase the acidity of low-acid foods and can also improve color and flavor.

Cold Pack - A canning procedure where raw food is placed in a jar. Also known as raw pack.

Enzymes - The proteins found in food that accelerate flavor, color, texture and nutritional changes once the food is cut, sliced, crushed, bruised or exposed to air. Enzymes are destroyed through proper blanching or hot-packing practices and will help improve food quality.

Exhausting - The removal of air from within and around food in a jar or canner. Blanching also exhausts air from live food tissues. Exhausting a pressure canner is necessary for the prevention of botulism risks in low-acid canned foods.

Fermentation - A change in food as a result of intentional bacteria growth, yeast or mold. Native bacteria can ferment natural sugars into lactic acid; a flavoring and preservative found in sauerkraut and naturally fermented dills. Other fermented foods include alcohol, vinegar, and some dairy products.

Heat Processing - Treating jars with sufficient heat to allow storing foods at normal temperatures.

Hermetic Seal - An airtight container seal that prevents reentry of air or microorganisms into packaged foods.

Hot Pack - Heating of raw food in boiling water or steam and placing it into hot jars.

Low-Acid Foods - Food that has little acid and a pH above 4.6. These foods don't have enough acid to prevent the growth of the bacterium Clostridium Botulinum. Low acid foods include vegetables, some tomatoes, figs, all meats, fish, seafood and some dairy foods. In order to control the risk of botulism, these foods need to be heat processed or acidified.

Microorganisms - Independent organisms that are microscopic in size. This includes bacteria, yeast, and mold. When in a suitable environment they can grow rapidly and can even divide or reproduce every ten to thirty minutes. This means they are able to reach a high population very quickly. Dangerous microorganisms can result in disease and food spoilage. Sometimes they can be intentionally added to ferment foods, make antibiotics and other reasons.

Mold - A fungus-type microorganism that results in a visible and colorful growth on food. Molds will grow on a variety of foods including acid foods such as jams and jellies as well as canned fruits. Heat processing and sealing will prevent growth on foods.

Mycotoxins - These are the toxins produced by mold growth on certain foods.

Open-Kettle Canning - This is a non-recommended method for canning. Food is heat processed in a covered kettle and then placed hot in sterile jars and sealed. Foods sealed in this way often have low vacuums and too much air, which causes a rapid loss of quality in foods. These foods will often spoil because they are recontaminated as the jars are filled.

Pasteurization - The act of heating certain foods enough to destroy heat-resistant pathogenic or disease-causing microorganisms that are typically associated with foods.

pH - A measure of alkalinity or acidity. The values range from 0 to 14. A food is considered neutral with a pH of 7.0. Lower numbers have more acid, and higher numbers have more alkalinity.

Pickling - This is the process of adding enough vinegar or lemon juice to a low-acid food to drop the pH to 4.6 or lower. Pickled foods can be safely heat processed in boiling water.

Pressure Canner - A specifically designed metal kettle with a lockable lid that can heat process low-acid food. They feature jar racks, one or more safety devices, systems for exhausting air and a way to measure and/or control pressure. The most common are canners with a capacity of 20 to 21 quarts. The minimum volume canner is 16-quart capacity or seven-quart jars. It isn't recommended to use any smaller capacity canner.

Raw Pack - The process of filling jars with raw, unheated food. Okay for canning low-acid foods, but will allow for quick loss of quality in acid foods that are heat processed in boiling water.

Spice Bag - A sealable fabric bag that extracts spice flavors in a pickling solution.

Spoilage - This is the result of undesirable bacteria, mold or other pathogen growth that can result in illness, injury or degrades the taste and/or qualities of foods.

Vacuum - A state of negative pressure. This reflects the thorough removal of air from within a jar of processed food. The higher the vacuum, the less air that is left in the jar. A vacuum doesn't guarantee that jars are sterile or safe.

Water Bath Canner - A large pot with a rack to hold jars. Acid foods such as fruits and tomatoes can be processed or canned in boiling water.

Yeasts - A group of microorganisms that reproduce by budding. They can be used in leavening bread and fermenting some foods.

RECIPES

PECTIN RECIPE

If you want to make the most natural and organic jam or jelly, then you can consider making your own pectin. Let's look at how you can make your own pectin at home.

Ingredients:

- 3 pounds washed and sliced tart green apples.
- 4 cups water
- 2 tablespoons lemon juice

Directions:

1. Wash but don't peel about seven large tart green apples. Crab Apples are best, but any tart apples will work.

2. Cut into pieces and place in a pot.

3. Add the water and lemon juice.

4. Boil until it is reduced by half; about 30 to 45 minutes.

5. Strain through a cheesecloth or jelly bag.

6. Boil the juice for another 20 minutes.

7. Pour into sanitized jars and seal them.

8. Store in the refrigerator, freezer or process in a water bath.

APPLE JELLY RECIPE

Ingredients:

- 6 pounds of apples (start a step 1 below) or 6 cups of apple juice (start at step 6 below)
- About 3 to 4 cups of water or apple juice for a stronger flavor.
- Your choice of sweetener.
- 1/2 teaspoon cinnamon.
- 1/2 packet of dry no-sugar added pectin.

Directions:

1. The most important thing is to choose the right apples. You want apples that are sweet, do not use sour apples. Some good ones to use are Red Delicious, Gala, Fuji and Rome. You should also use a mixture of these apples and not just a single

type. If you are simply going to start with apple juice, then make sure it is fresh, canned or frozen with no added sweeteners. If you are starting with apple juice, then skip to step 6 below.

2. Wash the apples in cold water and remove any stickers or labels. Then peel all the apples.

3. If you have an apple corer then use that, otherwise, use a paring knife to chop the apples. Make sure you remove seeds, hard parts, mush or dark areas.

4. Place three to four cups of water in the bottom of a large, thick-bottomed pot or about two inches of water in the pot. Place the lid on the pot and heat on high. Once it is boiling, turn it down to medium-high and add the apples. Cook until the apples are completely soft all the way through.

5. Place the soft cooked apples through a jelly strainer or pour them through a cheesecloth in a colander. If you don't mind chunky jelly you don't have to sieve the apples at all, simply allow the juice to stand for 20 minutes and then pour off the clear liquid to use. The sieve option allows you to

have clearer jelly. No matter what option you choose, you should have about six cups of apple juice.

6. Depending on the jelly you are making you will need to use a specific amount of sugar and pectin. Each brand of pectin will have its own directions. You can also use the following table to help guide you:

Type of Jelly	Type of Pectin	Sweetener
Regular	No Sugar or Regular	7 Cups Sugar
Low Sugar	No Sugar	4.5 Cups Sugar
Lower Sugar	No Sugar	2 Cups Sugar and 2 Cups Splenda
No Sugar	No Sugar	4 Cups Splenda
Natural	No Sugar	3 Cups Fruit Juice

7. In a small bowl, mix together about 1/4 cup of sweetener with the pectin. Remember that apple jelly often only requires 1/2 pack of pectin.

8. Stir the pectin mixture into the apple juice. Place the entire mix in a big pot on the stove over

medium to high heat. Stir often enough to prevent burning. It will take about five to ten minutes to reach a full boil.

9. Add the rest of the sugar once it has reached a full boil. Boil for 1 minute.

10. Test for jell thickness. Keep a metal tablespoon in a glass of ice water. Scoop a half spoonful of the mix and allow it to cool to room temperature on the spoon. If the thickness is what you want, then the jelly is ready. If it isn't right then, you can add more pectin and bring the ingredients to a boil for another minute.

11. Fill your canning jars 1/4 inch from the top and seal the lids. Can according to instructions.

12. Apple jelly can be stored 12 months and is safe to use that entire time. However, after 6 to 8 months the jelly will get darker in color and start to get runny. So for best results be sure to use within 6 months.

CHERRY JAM RECIPE

Ingredients:

- 3 pounds or 4 cups of chopped, pitted fresh cherries.

- 1.25 boxes of pectin.

- 2 tablespoons lemon juice if using sweet cherries, no lemon juice if you are using sour cherries.

- About 2.5 cups of sugar with sweet cherries and 4 cups of sugar with sour cherries.

Directions:

1. Pick the necessary cherries you need. Remember to only make your jam in small batches of about 4 cups at a time.

2. This recipe will result in about six, 8-ounce jars. You should start preparing your jars now, so they are ready for use later. You can use a dishwasher sanitize cycle, or you can use the hot water method to sanitize the jars and have them ready.

3. Wash your cherries and then remove the pits. You can do this with a cheap cherry pitter or do it

by hand depending on how much you have. Also, make sure you remove any stems and leaves. To prevent browning keep the cherries in a bowl with 1/4 lemon juice and cold water after pitting.

4. For cherry jam you want the cherries to be either finely chopped or ground. They don't need to be completely crushed, but at least mushed up some. When you do this, you will also be releasing the natural pectin. After chopping, you should have about 4 cups of cherries.

5. Measure out and prepare your sugar or sweetener. Mix the 1.25 boxes of pectin with 1/4 cup of sugar and set it aside.

6. Stir the pectin mix into the cherries and place in a large pot over medium to high heat, stirring often enough to keep it from burning. It often takes about 5 to 10 minutes to reach a full boil.

7. Once the mix has reached a full boil, add the rest of the sugar or sweetener and bring back to a boil for 1 minute. You can reduce foaming by bringing it to a boil slowly. Remove from heat after boiling for 1 minute.

8. Remove any excess foam from the top.

9. Test for thickness by using a metal tablespoon kept in a glass of ice water. Scoop a half spoonful of the mixture and allow it to cool to room temperature on the spoon. If it thickens to a consistency you like, then the jam is ready. If it isn't ready, you can add more pectin and boil for another minute.

10. Let it stand for five minutes and then stir completely. This will prevent the fruit from floating to the top of the jar but otherwise, won't affect the quality of the jam if you don't have time and have to skip this step.

11. Fill your jars within 1/4 inch of the top and seal. Then process according to canning instructions.

12. The jam is good for 12 months in storage. It can get darker in color and start to get runny after 6 to 8 months. So while it is good for 12 months, you should eat it within 6 months.

CHERRY JELLY RECIPE

Ingredients:

- 4 cups of cherry juice.

- 1.25 boxes of pectin.

- 2 tablespoon of lemon juice for sweet cherry jelly, none for sour cherries.

- About 3 to 4 cups of sugar with sweet cherries and 4 to 5 cups of sugar for sour cherries.

Directions:

1. Choose and pick your cherries. You will need about 4 cups of finely chopped and pitted cherries. As with jam, the jelly should only be made in small batches of about 4 cups at a time.

2. Start preparing your jars and lids, so you'll have them ready for later. A dishwasher on the sanitize cycle, or a hot water bath will work.

3. Wash the cherries in cold water and pit them using a cherry pitter or a knife. Make sure you remove any leaves and stems.

4. Finely chop or grind the cherries in a food processor, blender or juicer. Often 6 to 8 cups of cherries will yield 4 cups of juice. If needed, you can add water to make up the difference.

5. Place the cherries on the stove in a large pot over medium to high heat, stirring enough to prevent burning. Once it starts to boil, reduce the heat and allow to simmer for 10 minutes. If you used a juicer in step four you could skip to step seven, otherwise, continue.

6. Place the cooked cherries through a jelly strainer or through a cheesecloth in a colander. Sometimes jelly can form crystals. These don't affect taste and aren't harmful, but if you don't want them, then you should let the juice stand in a cool place overnight and straight through two thicknesses of damp cheesecloth to remove crystals.

7. Mix the pectin with 1/4 cup of sugar or sweetener. If you aren't using sugar, then you'll need to stir vigorously to prevent clumping of the pectin. Place the mix in a big pot over medium to high heat, stirring enough to prevent burning. It will take about 5 to 10 minutes to reach a full boil.

8. Once the mix has reached a full boil, add the rest of the sugar and boil for 1 minute. If you bring it to a boil slowly, then it will reduce foaming.

9. Skim any excess foam off the top.

10. Test for thickness using a metal tablespoon sitting in a glass of ice water. Scoop a half spoonful of mix and allow it to come to room temperature. If it thickens to a consistency you like, then the jelly is done. If not you can add more pectin and bring to a boil for one minute.

11. Allow it to stand for five minutes and stir completely if you want to prevent the fruit from floating to the top.

12. Fill jars 1/4 inch from the top and seal. Follow canning instructions.

13. Jelly is good for 12 months in storage. After 6 to 8 months it can get darker in color and runny. Although still safe to eat, it is best to consume within 6 months.

FIG JELLY RECIPE

Ingredients:

- About 2 dozen large figs such as Brown Turkey or 40 smaller figs such as Celeste. Basically you want about three to five pounds of figs.
- 1/4 cup lemon juice.
- 1/2 cup water
- 1/4 teaspoon cinnamon
- 1 package or 8 tablespoons pectin.
- About 4.5 cups of sugar or your choice of sweetener.

Directions:

1. Select and choose the figs you want to use and make sure you have enough to complete the recipe.

2. Sterilize your jars and lids either in the dishwasher or in a boiling water process and have them ready for canning later.

3. Wash the figs and cut off the stems and bottoms. You don't need to peel the figs unless you want to.

Then slice up the figs. Once you're done, you should have four to five cups of figs.

4. Measure out your choice of sweetener. Use the following table to help guide you in how much sweetener to add:

Type of Jam	Type of Pectin	Sweetener
Regular	No Sugar or Regular	7 Cups Sugar
Low Sugar	No Sugar	4.5 Cups Sugar
Lower Sugar	No Sugar	2 Cups Sugar and 2 Cups Splenda
No Sugar	No Sugar	4 Cups Splenda
Natural	No Sugar	3 Cups Fruit Juice

5. Mix the dry pectin with 1/4 cup of your choice of sweetener.

6. Mix the figs with the pectin mixture, water and lemon juice in a pot on the stove.

7. Add the rest of sugar once the mixture reaches a full boil and then boil for one minute.

8. Skim the foam from the top.

9. Test for thickness. Use a metal tablespoon sitting in a glass of ice water. Scoop a half spoonful and allow to cool to room temperature. If you like the consistency then the jelly is ready, otherwise, add more pectin and boil for another minute before testing again.

10. Allow the jelly to stand for five minutes and then stir completely to prevent the fruit from floating to the top of your jars.

11. Fill your jars within 1/4 from the top and seal.

12. Can according to instructions.

13. Fig jelly can be stored and good for 18 months. After eighteen months the jelly will get darker in color and runny. For best quality, you should use within 12 months.

PEACH AND NECTARINE RECIPE

Ingredients:

- About 3.5 pounds of whole peaches or nectarines, totaling about 5-6 cups of peeled, chopped fruit.
- 1/4 cup lemon juice.
- 1/2 cup water.
- About 4.5 cups of sugar or another sweetener.
- 1 package or 8 tablespoons pectin.

Directions:

1. Choose your peaches or nectarines and make sure you have enough for the ingredients.

2. For jams, you should only make in small batches of about 6 cups at a time.

3. Prepare your jars now, so you don't rush later. If you have a dishwasher with the sanitize cycle, start the jars now. If you don't have a dishwasher that can do it, then use the water bath processing method. Wash the containers in hot, soapy water

and rinse before boiling for ten minutes and keeping them in hot water until you use them.

4. Wash the fruit. Remove any stems, leaves and soft or mushy parts. Drain the water off in a colander.

5. Peel the fruit.

6. Cut the fruits, removing any brown spots and mushy areas. Remove pits and leave in halves or quarters. Then mush up the fruit slightly.

7. Sprinkle 1/4 cup lemon juice in the bowl of fruit to keep them from turning brown. Stir to make sure all surfaces are coated with lemon juice.

8. Depending on the type of jam/jelly you're making measure out your choice of sweetener and pectin. Each box of pectin will have its own instructions and directions. Otherwise, use the table below:

Type of Jam	Type of Pectin	Sweetener
Regular	No Sugar or Regular	7 Cups of Sugar

Low Sugar	No Sugar	4.5 Cups of Sugar
Lower Sugar	No Sugar	2 Cups Sugar and 2 cups Splenda
No Sugar	No Sugar	4 Cups Splenda
Natural	No Sugar	3 Cups Fruit Juice

9. Mix the pectin with about 1/4 cup of your sweetener.

10. Stir the pectin mixture into the fruit and add 1/2 cup of water. Place in a large pot over medium to high heat and stir often enough to prevent burning. It often takes about 5 to 10 minutes to reach a full boil.

11. Add the rest of the sweetener and bring to a boil and boil for 1 minute.

12. Test for thickness by using a metal tablespoon sitting in a glass of ice water. Scoop a half spoonful and allow it to cool to room temperature. If it thickens to a consistency you like, then the jam/jelly is ready. If not then add more pectin and bring to a boil for 1 minute.

13. Fill your jars with 1/4 inch room at the top. Place lid and ring on them before following canning instructions.

14. The jam/jelly can be stored for up to 12 months. After 6 to 8 months they will become darker in color and be slightly runny. Although still safe to eat, it is best to eat them within 6 months.

PEAR RECIPE

Makes about 8-9, 8-ounce jars

Ingredients:

- 6 pounds of pears or 6 cups of pear juice
- 1/2 teaspoon cinnamon

Directions:

1. Choose the appropriate pears, I find it is best to choose sweet pears, so you don't have to add sugar. If you are going to use pear juice for this recipe, then skip to step 6.

2. Make sure you have the appropriate 6 pounds of pears unless you are going to use pear juice to make this recipe.

3. Wash the pears in plain cold water, remove any stickers or labels. Once washed peel them.

4. Chop up the pears. Remove any seeds, hard parts, mushing areas or dark spots.

5. Place the pears in about 1 inch of water on the bottom of a huge, thick-bottomed pot. Turn on high heat and put the lid on the pot. Once it is boiling,

turn it down to medium-high until the pears are thoroughly soft.

6. Determine whether you want to make pear jam or jelly.

   a) For pear jelly you need to filter, sieve or strain the pears. You can use a jelly strainer or pour them through a cheesecloth in a colander. Make sure you have about 6 cups of juice.

   b) For pear jam, you will use a food mill. If you don't have a food mill, you can simply stir the cooked pears or strain them. The main thing is to make sure you separate any remaining skins, seeds, hard parts or stems.

7. Depending on the type of jam or jelly you're making you will need a different amount of sugar and/or type of pectin. Each type of pectin will have specific directions inside the box. The following chart will give you an idea of what you need to add:

Type of Jam	Type of Pectin	Sweetener
Regular	Regular	7 cups of sugar

Lower Sugar	Lower Sugar	4.5 cups of sugar
Lowest Sugar	No Sugar	4 cups Splenda
Lower Sugar	Lower Sugar or No Sugar	2 cups sugar and 2 cups Splenda
No Sugar	No Sugar	4 cups Splenda
Natural	No Sugar	3 cups fruit juice

8. In a small bowl, mix the dry pectin with about 1/4 of your sweetener. If you aren't using sugar, you'll have to stir vigorously to prevent clumping.

9. Stir the pectin into the pear juice and place in a large pot on the stove over medium to high heat. Stir as often as needed to prevent from burning. It often takes five to ten minutes to bring to a full boil.

10. Once it has reached a full boil, add the rest of the sweetener and then bring back to a boil and allow to boil for one minute.

11. Use a metal tablespoon in a glass of ice water. Take a half a spoon of the mix and allow it to cool to room temperature on the spoon. If it thickens to

a consistency you like, then your jam is ready. If it isn't then add some more pectin and boil for another minute.

12. Fill your jars within 1/4 inch of the top, seat the lid and tighten the ring.

13. Following directions for canning the jam/jelly.

14. Once your jars are cool, you can store them for up to 12 months. After six to eight months you may notice them getting darker in color and slightly runny. At this time they are still safe to eat, but may not taste as good or have a grainy texture. For best texture and taste you need to eat within the first six months.

BREAD AND BUTTER PICKLE RECIPE

Ingredients:

- 6 pounds of 4 to 5-inch pickling cucumbers
- 8 cups thinly sliced onions
- 1/2 cup canning or pickling salt
- 4 cups vinegar
- 4 1/2 cups sugar
- 2 tablespoons mustard seed
- 1 1/2 tablespoons celery seed
- 1 tablespoon ground turmeric
- 1 cup pickling lime

Directions:

Wash the cucumbers and cut 1/16 inch off the blossom end and discard. Cut into 3/16 inch slices.

Combine cucumber and onion in a large bowl. Add salt. Cover with 2 inches crushed or cubed ice. Refrigerate three to four hours and add more ice as needed.

Combine the rest of the ingredients in a large pot. Boil for ten minutes.

Drain and add cucumbers and onions, then slowly reheat to boiling.

Fill jars with slices and cooking syrup, leaving 1/2 inch headspace.

Seal jars and process with low-temperature pasteurization or according to the table below for processing in a boiling-water canner.

Once processed they should be stored four to five weeks to develop ideal flavor.

Pack Style	Jar Size	0-1,000 ft. Altitude	1,001-6,000 ft. Altitude	Above 6,000 ft. Altitude
Hot	Pints or Quarts	10 minutes	15 minutes	20 minutes

FRESH PACK DILL PICKLES RECIPE

Ingredients:

- 8 pounds 3 to 5-inch pickling cucumbers
- 2 gallons water
- 1 1/4 cups canning or pickling salt
- 1 1/2 quarts vinegar
- 1/4 cup sugar
- 2 quarts water
- 2 tablespoons whole mixed pickling spice
- 3 tablespoons whole mustard seed
- 4 1/2 tablespoons dill seed

Directions:

Wash cucumbers and cut 1/16 inch slice off the blossom end and discard, but least 1/4 inch of stem attached.

Dissolve 3/4 cup salt in 2 gallons water. Pour over cucumbers and let stand for 12 hours then drain.

Combine vinegar, 1/2 cup salt, sugar and 2 quarts water. Add mixed pickling spices tied in a clean white cloth. Heat to boiling.

Fill jars with cucumbers. Add 1 teaspoon mustard seed and 1 1/2 teaspoons dill seed per pint.

Cover cucumbers with boiling pickling solution, leaving 1/2 inch headspace.

Seal jars and process with the low-temperature pasteurization treatment or according to the table below for a boiling-water canner.

Pack Style	Jar Size	0-1,000 ft. Altitude	1,001-6,000 ft. Altitude	Above 6,000 ft. Altitude
Raw	Pints	10 minutes	15 minutes	20 minutes
Raw	Quarts	15 minutes	20 minutes	25 minutes

SWEET GHERKIN PICKLES RECIPE

Ingredients:

- 7 pounds 1 and 1/2 inch or fewer cucumbers
- 1/2 cup canning or pickling salt
- 8 cups sugar
- 6 cups vinegar
- 3/4 teaspoon turmeric
- 2 teaspoons celery seeds
- 2 teaspoons whole mixed pickling spice
- 2 cinnamon sticks

Directions:

Wash cucumbers and cut 1/16 inch off the blossom end and discard. Leave 1/4 inch of stem attached.

Place cucumbers in a large container and cover with boiling water.

Six to eight hours later, drain and cover with 6 quarts of fresh boiling water with 1/4 cup salt. Do this for two days.

On the third day, drain and prick cucumbers with a table fork.

Combine 3 cups vinegar, 3 cups sugar, turmeric, and spices; bring to a boil.

Pour over cucumbers. Six to eight hours later, drain and save the pickling syrup.

Add 2 cups sugar and 2 cups vinegar, reheat to a boil. Pour over pickles.

On the fourth day, drain and save syrup. Add another 2 cups sugar and 1 cup vinegar. Heat to boiling and pour over pickles.

Six to eight hours later, drain and save pickling syrup.

Add 1 cup sugar and heat to boiling.

Fill pint jars with pickles and cover with hot syrup, leaving 1/2 inch headspace.

Seal jars and process with the low-temperature pasteurization method or according to the table below for boiling-water canners.

| Pack | Jar | 0-1,000 | 1,001- | Above |

Style	Size	ft. Altitude	6,000 ft. Altitude	6,000 ft. Altitude
Raw	Pints	5 minutes	10 minutes	15 minutes

QUICK SWEET PICKLES RECIPE

Ingredients:

- 8 pounds 3 to 4-inch pickling cucumbers
- 1/3 cup canning or pickling salt
- 4 1/2 cups sugar
- 3 1/2 cups vinegar
- 2 teaspoons celery seed
- 1 tablespoon whole allspice
- 2 tablespoons mustard seed
- 1 cup pickling lime

Directions:

Wash cucumbers and cut 1/16 inch off the blossom end and discard. Leave 1/4 inch of stem attached. Slice or cut into strips if wanted.

Place cucumbers in a bowl and sprinkle with 1/3 cup salt. Cover with 2 inches of crushed or cubed ice. Refrigerate three to four hours, adding more ice as needed. Drain well.

Combine sugar, vinegar, celery seed, allspice and mustard seed in a 6-quart kettle and heat to boiling.

For a hot pack - Add cucumbers and heat slowly until solution returns to a boil. Stir occasionally to heat evenly. Fill jars, leaving 1/2 inch headspace.

For a raw pack - Fill jars with cucumber and leave 1/2 inch headspace. Add hot pickling syrup and leave 1/2 inch headspace. Seal and process with the low-temperature pasteurization method or according to the table below.

Pack Style	Jar Size	0-1,000 ft. Altitude	1,001-6,000 ft. Altitude	Above 6,000 ft. Altitude

Hot	Pints or Quarts	5 minutes	10 minutes	15 minutes
Raw	Pints	10 minutes	15 minutes	20 minutes
Raw	Quarts	15 minutes	20 minutes	25 minutes

REDUCED SODIUM SLICED SWEET PICKLES RECIPE

Ingredients:

- 4 pounds 3 to 4-inch pickling cucumbers

Brining Solution:

- 1 quart distilled white vinegar
- 1 tablespoon canning or pickling salt
- 1 tablespoon mustard seed
- 1/2 cup sugar

Canning Syrup:

- 1 2/3 cups distilled white vinegar
- 3 cups sugar

- 1 tablespoon whole allspice
- 2 1/4 teaspoon celery seed

Directions:

Wash cucumbers and cut 1/16 inch off the blossom end and discard. Cut cucumbers into 1/4 inch slices.

Combine all canning syrup ingredients in a saucepan and bring to boil. Keep syrup hot until used.

Mix the brining solution ingredients in a large kettle. Add the cut cucumbers, cover and simmer until the cucumbers change color to dull green, about five to seven minutes.

Drain the cucumber slices and then fill the jars. Cover with hot canning syrup and leave 1/2 inch headspace. Seal jars and process in a boiling-water canner according to the table below.

Pack Style	Jar Size	0-1,000 ft. Altitude	1,001-6,000 ft. Altitude	Above 6,000 ft. Altitude
Hot	Pints	10	15	20

		minutes	minutes	minutes

PICKLED BREAD AND BUTTER ZUCCHINI RECIPE

Ingredients:

- 16 cups fresh sliced zucchini
- 4 cups thinly sliced onions
- 1/2 cup canning or pickling salt
- 4 cups white vinegar
- 2 cups sugar
- 4 tablespoons mustard seed
- 2 tablespoons celery seed
- 2 teaspoons ground turmeric

Directions:

Cover the zucchini and onion slips with 1 inch of water and salt. Allow to stand two hours and then drain thoroughly.

Combine vinegar, sugar, and spices. Bring to a boil and add zucchini and onions. Simmer for 5 minutes.

Fill jars, leaving 1/2 inch headspace. Seal jars and process with low-temperature pasteurization method or according to the table below for a boiling-water canner.

Pack Style	Jar Size	0-1,000 ft. Altitude	1,001-6,000 ft. Altitude	Above 6,000 ft. Altitude
Hot	Pints or Quarts	10 minutes	15 minutes	20 minutes

PICKLED ASPARAGUS RECIPE

Ingredients:

- 7 pounds asparagus
- 7 large garlic cloves
- 3 cups water
- 3 cups white distilled vinegar
- 1/3 cup canning salt
- 2 teaspoons dill seed

Directions:

Wash, rinse and sterilize your canning jars. Keep hot until ready to use.

Wash asparagus gently and fully under running water. Cut stems from the bottom, leaving spears with tips that will fit into the jar with 1/2 inch headspace.

Peel and wash garlic cloves. Place a garlic clove at the bottom of each jar and then tightly pack the asparagus with blunt ends on the bottom.

Combine water, vinegar, salt and dill seed in an 8-quart saucepot or Dutch oven. Bring to a boil. Pour boiling hot pickling brine over the spears, leaving 1/2 inch headspace.

Seal jars and process according to the boiling-water canner table below. Allow to cool, undisturbed for 12 to 24 hours and then check the seal.

Allow to sit for three to five days before eating for best flavor.

Pack Style	Jar Size	0-1,000 ft. Altitude	1,001-6,000 ft. Altitude	Above 6,000 ft. Altitude
Raw	12-ounce jars	10 minutes	15 minutes	20 minutes

PICKLED CARROTS RECIPE

Ingredients:

- ➢ 2 3/4 pounds peeled carrots
- ➢ 5 1/2 cups white distilled vinegar
- ➢ 1 cup water

- 2 cups sugar
- 2 teaspoons canning salt
- 8 teaspoons mustard seed
- 4 teaspoons celery seed

Directions:

Wash and rinse your canning jars. Sterilize and keep hot until ready to use.

Wash and peel carrots. Wash again after peeling and cut into rounds about 1/2 inch thick.

Combine vinegar, water, sugar and canning salt in an 8-quart stockpot or Dutch oven. Bring to boil and gently boil for 3 minutes. Add carrots and bring back to boil. Reduce heat and simmer until the carrots are half cooked about 10 minutes.

Place 2 teaspoons mustard seed and 1 teaspoon celery seed in the bottom of each pint jar.

Fill the hot jars with hot carrots, leaving 1-inch headspace. Cover with the hot pickling liquid and leave 1/2 inch headspace. Seal the jars.

Process in a boiling-water canner according to the table below. Allow jars to cool, undisturbed for 12 to 24 hours and then check the seal.

For best flavor development, allow to sit for three to five days before eating.

Pack Style	Jar Size	0-1,000 ft. Altitude	1,001-6,000 ft. Altitude	Above 6,000 ft. Altitude
Hot	Pints	15 minutes	20 minutes	25 minutes

PICKLED FIGS RECIPE

Ingredients:

- 4 quarts firm-ripe figs
- 3 cups sugar
- 2 quarts water
- 2 cups sugar
- 3 cups vinegar
- 2 sticks cinnamon

- 1 tablespoon whole allspice
- 1 tablespoon whole cloves

Directions:

Peel figs or if using unpeeled, pour boiling water over the figs and let stand until cool and then drain.

Add 3 cups sugar to water and cook until dissolved.

Add figs and cook slowly for 30 minutes.

Add 2 cups sugar and vinegar. Tie spices in a cheesecloth bag and add to figs. Cook gently until the figs are clear.

Cover and let stand 12 to 24 hours in the refrigerator.

Remove the spice bag and heat figs in brine until boiling.

Place in jars, leaving 1/2 inch headspace. Seal and process in a boiling water canner based on the table below.

Pack	Jar	0-1,000 ft.	1,001-3,000	3,001-6,000	Above

Style	Size	Altitude	ft. Altitude	ft. Altitude	6,000 ft. Altitude
Hot	Pints	15 minutes	20 minutes	20 minutes	20 minutes

Made in the USA
Middletown, DE
30 March 2017